MW01489918

EFFECTIVE!

Learning to Lead Yourself Well

S. M. Wibberley

Edifying Services Press
www.edifyingservices.com

Other books by S. M. Wibberley

EQUIPPED! Twelve Empowering Truths and How to Use Them
formerly *Ready for Everyday Spiritual Warfare* (2012)
and *Knowing Jesus is Enough for Joy, Period!* (2010)

*EDIFIED! 365 Devotionals to Stimulate Personal Worship and
Spark Inner Transformation* (2013)

From Canterbury to the Ends of the Earth and Back (2014)
The Memoirs of a Connecticut Yankee's Spiritual Journey

Available at www.edifyingservices.com and some at Amazon.com

Copyright © 2013 S.M. Wibberley

Unless otherwise indicated, artwork copyright © Nathanael
Wibberley. Used by permission.

Printed in United States of America

ISBN 978-0-9832077-5-7

All rights reserved solely by the author. The author guarantees that,
to his knowledge, all contents are original and do not infringe upon
the legal rights of any other person or work. No part of this book
may be reproduced in any form without the permission of the
author. The views expressed in this book are not necessarily those
of the publisher.

Unless otherwise marked, Scripture quotations are taken from the
Holy Bible, New International Version®. Copyright © 1973,
1978,1984 by International Bible Society. Used by permission of
the International Bible Society.

"NIV" and "New International Version" are trademarks registered
in the United States Patent and Trademark Office by International
Bible Society.

Dedicated to

Dave and Mitzy Shinen
My first Spiritual Mentors

And

Sig and Helen Kristiansen
My first Pastor and his wife after my new birth

www.edifyingserives.com

Contents

Introduction 9

Chapter 1   Why is Self-leadership Important? 12

Chapter 2   What Does "Leading Yourself Well" Look Like? 16

Chapter 3   The Biblical Basis 20

Chapter 4   What's a Worldview Got To Do With It? 27

Chapter 5   What Does It Mean To Lead Yourself Well
Spiritually? 34

Chapter 6   What Can I Do to Nurture My First Love for Jesus? 39

Chapter 7   What Does It Mean To Lead Yourself Well
Intellectually? 45

Chapter 8   What Does It Mean To Lead Yourself Well
Volitionally? 51

Chapter 9   What Does It Mean To Lead Yourself Well
Emotionally? 60

Chapter 10   How Can I Lead Myself Well Emotionally? 69

Chapter 11   What Does It Mean To Lead Yourself Well
Physically? 78

Chapter 12   What Does It Mean To Lead Yourself Well
Financially? 83

Check your records and see if you are actually giving a minimum
of 10% of your income to the Lord. If not, begin to do so 86

Chapter 13   What Does It Mean To Lead Yourself Well Socially?
.... 87

Chapter 14   So, What's Next? 92

Chapter 15   How can I expand my obedience? 95

Appendix A   Meditation 99

Appendix B   Examples of Personal Worship 105

Appendix C Praying On the Armor of Ephesians 6:10-18 109

Introduction

The master craftsman looked up from his work to see the little boy standing in the doorway. He smiled. "Come here, son," he said. "Help me in my work." What could such a small boy do to help in the work of a skilled craftsman? Nothing of importance we'd say.

Yet the master drew the boy to his side saying, "Sit with me here and watch what I'm doing. See how I am shaping this piece to fit in that spot? Now, when I need another tool you can hand it to me and then take the one I just finished with and put in its place. See how they are arranged here on the bench?" And he went on to name each tool and tell of its use.

So it is with God and us, His children. One of His primary desires is that we partner with Him in His great plan for the universe. We see this consistently through Scripture as He prepares things for his people and then invites them to join Him in His work.

This starts right in the beginning when, after preparing the world, God created Adam and Eve in His image, making them able to participate with Him in His work. He gave them specific instructions on what to do: *"...fill the earth and subdue it. Rule over the fish of the sea and the birds of the air and over every living creature that moves on the ground"* (Gen. 1:28). And what not to do: *"...you must not eat from the tree of the knowledge of good and evil, for when you eat of it you will surely die"* (Gen. 2:16,17).

Then He waited for them to lead themselves well, living and working within His directives. However, as we know, both of them led themselves poorly, taking the whole universe off track with their disobedience. Failure to lead ourselves well is a deadly serious decison.

In spite of the fall, God did not give up on calling people to partner with Him. Today He continues to call us to lead ourselves well and join Him in what He's doing. A search on the phrase "let us" in the Epistles shows how often He expresses this invitation: 46 times. Galatians 5:25 is a good example: *"Since we live by the Spirit, let us keep in step with the Spirit."*

Leading ourselves well is, very simply, obeying God. Each day we have multiple opportunities to do what Adam and Eve did not do: deny self and obey God. Will we respond to His invitations and commands with obedience? Or will we just drift along, led by our culture, our friends or our heart?

In this book we are going to look at how we can lead ourselves well in seven foundational areas: the spiritual, intellectual, volitional, emotional, physical, financial and social dimensions of our lives. There are, of course, more areas we could cover, but these seven are the major ones and will influence what we do in any other area we might consider.

We will take two "passes" through them. The first and longer part will lay out the concepts and principles involved, along with what I consider to be the single most important aspect of leading ourselves well in each area. The last chapter of the book will be the second "pass," taking a wider look at each level, giving more examples of leading ourselves well in these different areas.

You will see how the positives of one area cascade down into the succeeding levels: leading yourself well in the initial areas will definitely change how you do things in the other levels.

May you be encouraged and equipped to lead yourself well in following Jesus.

Effectiveness Defined.

Chapter 1   Why is Self-leadership Important?

Lillias Trotter turned in her camel's saddle and looked back at the mountains of Algeria behind her. She had spent the last three months journeying through this rough territory with her ministry partner and Bedouin guides. This trip had been difficult beyond the normal trials of travel in a desert country. As they'd gone from one remote village to another in order to share the gospel, they found that the police had gone before them, telling each village that two white witches were coming. They warned the villagers, commanding them, "Don't believe anything they say!"

Such obstacles were nothing new to Lillias Trotter; through the years of work in that difficult land she had learned to trust God to work through such opposition. "God always has a sequel!" she was fond of saying.

She had such a perspective of God and His sovereignty because she had led herself well, starting with leaving behind the privileges of her wealthy English family and the prestige of being one of the outstanding artists in Europe in the late 1800s. Turning from this, she gave her life to working in the obscurity and difficulty of North Africa. She laid aside the values of her culture and took up the values of God's Word. And she had lived these values daily in the difficult, smelly and resistant conditions of Algeria in the late 1800s and early 1900s.

Listen to this astounding description of what she called a "trained faith."

> Trained faith is a triumphant gladness in having nothing but God—no rest, no foothold, nothing but Himself—a triumphant gladness in swinging out into that abyss, rejoicing in a very fresh emergency that is going to prove Him true—the Lord Alone. That is trained faith.[1]

---

[1] *A Passion for the Impossible: The Life of Lillias Trotter* by Miriam Huffman Rockness

Such a trained faith is the result of a life well led, a life that continues to impact others long after death, as does Lillias Trotter's.

This is God's Desire

The Bible is full of commands to lead ourselves well. For instance Psalm 34:13,14 says, *"keep your tongue from evil and your lips from speaking lies. Turn from evil and do good; seek peace and pursue it."* If we do these things we will be obeying, pleasing and joining God in His work.

We are called upon to make many decisions each day, like in the following situation.

"Hello, is Frank there? What, he just left and won't be back for a week? But I need to get some information from him today! Any chance of reaching him? Does he have a cell phone? No. Any suggestions? Well thanks anyway."

We can respond to this situation by complaining, worrying and fretting. Or we can lead ourselves well by giving thanks to God for allowing this, praising Him for how He will work it out and asking Him for wisdom in how to proceed. In each response we give throughout the day, whether we know it or not, we are leading ourselves for good or ill.

The concept of leading yourself well came to me as the result of taking a seminar called, *Leading Like Jesus.*[2] Leading yourself was just one very small part of the seminar, but stood out to me as significant. It was pointed out that leadership actually has four spheres. I liken these to a baseball diamond.

First base is leading yourself. Everyone has been given the responsibility to lead him or herself; we need to do it wisely and well, learning to make good decisions in every area of life. This gives perspective, develops 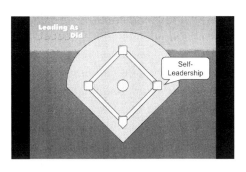 responsibility and provides opportunity to be an example.

---

[2] I do not recommend all the materials written or endorsed by the author of this seminar, but found this one helpful.

If we learn to lead ourselves well, then we are equipped to go on to second base, which is leading others one-on-one. The fact is, we are all leaders whether we have an official position or not—people around us look to us for example and encouragement or for excuses they can utilize.

Leading one-on-one simply means teaching others to do what we've been doing in our own life. It is leading from integrity (doing what we say we believe) and it develops trust. This is the basis of any discipleship or mentoring relationship. It is what a pastor should be doing with his elders and future leaders. It is what older believers should be doing with newer ones. It is what a

husband should be doing for his wife, and both mother and father should be doing for their children, one at a time, teaching them to be effective.

Leading well one-on-one can open

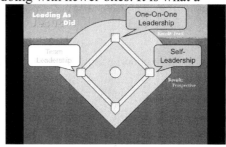

the way to go to third base, which is leading a team or small group. Here we apply in a group setting the principles we've been teaching one-on-one. If I've led myself well, I will seek to use the team's projects to develop my teammates, instead of using my teammates to develop my projects.[3] I will help them to lead themselves well and to lead others well one-on-one. A father should be doing this for his whole family, the basic small group of society. Anyone can do this with his or her friends and colleagues, or leading a committee or team. Doing this well develops community.

If we lead well in the small group setting, we may be offered the opportunity to be in organizational leadership. Since we are practiced in leading well in the other areas, we are now equipped to bring effectiveness for God to many people. This

---

[3] This concept was gleaned from another source which I have forgotten and could not locate in internet searches.

could be some role in the church, in the community or in a Christian organization where we apply what we have learned in the other three areas of leadership.

We must remember that it all starts with first base: *leading yourself* well. If you don't get to first base, you can't go on. It's foundational to all else in life. Don't skip first base! Learn to lead yourself well!

Chapter 2   What Does "Leading Yourself Well" Look Like?

After knocking on the door, I let myself in and went down the hall to Ken's TV room, treading gingerly on the encrusted carpet, caked with mud, wood bark and dog hair. Ken looked up from his easy chair. He was wedged in the corner behind his card table piled high with old mail, magazines, medicine and miscellaneous debris.

"Hi," I said. "Just stopped by to see how you are. How goes it today?"

"Not too well," replied Ken, looking down at his breakfast of greasy home fries. He rested the bowl on his bulging stomach and coughed, "I'm really dizzy this morning. Probably my diabetes acting up again. Haven't been watching my blood sugar much lately."

He didn't look too well either, with hair sticking out every which way, his beard frizzy and his clothes all rumpled. They--and he--obviously hadn't been washed in quite a while, judging from the strong odor he gave off.

He didn't ask me to sit down, but I looked around for a spot anyway. Both his couches and the armchair were all filled to overflowing with a hodge-podge of items, so I just pushed back some of the debris and made a little spot to perch on.

Reaching over to the windowsill Ken picked up his Bible and Daily Bread. "I was just fixing to do my daily reading. Do you want to join me?" he asked.

"Sure," I said.

As Ken read, his dog heaved himself up and waddled over so I could give him a scratching. The fat grey cat soon followed. Listening to Ken I glanced around as I petted them. There were piles of dog and cat hair along the wall. The huge TV screen had empty cans and bottles as well as VCR tapes piled high on it. Clothes were draped on the backs of the couches and piled on the floor next to a chain saw and gas can.

When Ken finished reading we talked about cutting some firewood together. After praying I left him to his TV.

****

The bank vice president strode toward me and reached out his hand. "Jerry Smith," he said, "Glad to meet you, Steve! Have a

16

seat." He gestured towards an armchair as he walked behind his desk.

Although he was probably in his 50s, Jerry was still slim and trim. He was well dressed with suit, tie, shiny shoes and his desk looked the same: neat, orderly, not a speck of dust in sight.

"Would you like something to drink? Coffee, tea….?"

"I'll have some water, thanks," I replied. Jerry made a phone call and then turned to me, smiling.

"So, you are interested in a loan," he said, more than asked.

"Yes, I'm thinking about one. I have three questions that I hope you can answer."

"Fire away," Jerry replied. But before I could begin there was a knock on the door. Jerry opened it and took the glass of water from the lady, bringing it to me. "There you go," he said.

"Thanks," I replied. I asked my questions. Jerry answered them immediately and knowledgably. I drank my water and left fully informed, able to make a wise decision.

****

Looking at my encounters with these two very different men--actual encounters with real acquaintances of mine--I want to ask this question, "Which one is leading himself well?"

Clearly Ken's life is completely in shambles, while Jerry is disciplined, successful and probably near the top of his career. He is doing a much better job of leading himself well in almost every area. I say almost because there is a hint that Ken may be ahead of Jerry in one way. Jerry showed no interest in spiritual things, while Ken made it a point to read his Bible each day, even though he is not a follower of Christ, yet. It remains to be seen where that leads, but hopefully to a full surrender to God—and that could bring change in the whole of Ken's life!

Most of us would much rather be in Jerry's shoes than Ken's. So what's made the difference between these two men? Why did they end up in these very disparate conditions?

Stages of Life

The truth is, we do what we actually value, not what we claim to believe. My first team leader in the Middle East used to say, "Old age is lived out of the treasure chest of your youth." That is, the values and habits we select and adopt in our earlier life become stronger and stronger as we get older, shaping our later years. If we opt for complaining and indulging or for giving thanks and being disciplined, these choices will guide us more and more as life goes on.

We adopt, adapt and practice these values through different stages of life. As I've observed in my own life and in the lives of those around me, after childhood there are, in general, seven discernable stages.

When we are teen-agers we are trying to figure out who we are.

In our 20s we are trying out and selecting values.

At 30 we become adults (there is a definite shift at this age, a solidification which signals actual, responsible adulthood beginning; if you've been there, you know what I'm talking about).

In our 30s we tend to work hard, living out the values we have selected, relying on our natural strength, our talents, training and experience. We enjoy the challenge and revel in being able to meet it. Our hopes draw us on to the future.

Then if we mature properly, around the time we turn 40 we will shift to working smart. This means learning to delegate, to be more selective in how we use our resources. It means we have learned we don't have all the answers and need to work together with others. If we are followers of Jesus, it means we will pray more and strive less. We learn to be more focused on what is important, realizing we will probably not achieve all we'd hoped for—and that's ok as long as we do what God considers important.

In our 50s we should be putting more time into mentoring others.

In our 60s we should be stepping back and giving room to those we've mentored, and perhaps writing about the things we've learned.

In our 70s and 80s we should be acting as life coaches and making prayer our primary work.

Such positive development results from many choices we make along the way. We won't always make good ones--no one gets it right all the time--but if in general we are leading ourselves well, we can recover from the poor ones and learn from our mistakes.

Unfortunately many people make a long series of destructively negative choices and end up like Ken. As my father would say, there are two kinds of people, those who live (like Ken) and those who live and learn (like Jerry).

Making a long series of uncorrected poor value choices as Ken did, means you will probably miss the transition from working hard to working smart. The lure of success, the lust for significance, the rush you get from having control of events and people as well as the feeling of accomplishment in doing it yourself—these all seduce you into relying on your own gifting and training plus your physical and mental capacities alone rather than delegating, teaming and streamlining.

However, strength levels begin to decline after 40, at first imperceptibly, then at a greater rate. This leaves hard workers in their later years without the resources they need to perform well by just working hard. In contrast those who made the switch to working smart are wisely able to engage the strengths of those around them so they can be productive right to the end.

Knowing Where We Are in the Process

One important key in our development in life is having a way of measuring choices before we make them. It is possible to lead ourselves well only if we have valid standards to go by. In this book we are going to use biblical standards to measure decisions. These standards are the insight of the ages, the writings of the sages but more importantly, the wisdom of God. As the Creator, God has give us His "user manual" where He has revealed what we need to know in making wise choices. These standards have been tried and proven over the centuries and millenniums to be valid, trustable and powerful—because God knows what He is doing. Our primary model in this is Jesus, the One who led Himself better than any other human being.

As mentioned in the introduction, we will look at seven areas of self-leadership: spiritual, intellectual, volitional, emotional, physical, financial and social. If we lead ourselves well in these seven areas, our lives will continually be on an upward trajectory.

Chapter 3   The Biblical Basis

Second Peter chapter one gives us a Scriptural basis for leading ourselves well. Peter also gives us a clear road map of how to do it. The seven qualities he lists in 2 Peter 1:5-7 coincide well with the seven areas that we will cover.

As a side note, these verses also contain some of the most astounding statements in the whole Bible concerning our position as followers of Christ. Before we look at the wonderful words of this passage, let me make three observations about Peter's writing.

First is the power of certainty that rings out through these verses: "we *have* received....*have* been given....He *has* given everything we need....*has* given us very great and precious promises....you will *never* fall.... *will* receive." Strong, clear statements of biblical fact we can rely on.

Second is the frequent use of the word "through." Peter tells us clearly through what we can receive or have already received the gifts he mentions and how we can continue to receive what we need. Watch for these "throughs" in the passage as we discuss it.

Third are the strong and direct statements of who Jesus is-- proclaiming definitively the deity of Christ.

So, let's go through this passage together. Significant words will be in normal font instead of italics. I will make comments throughout.

2 Peter 1:1 *"Simon Peter, a servant and apostle of Jesus Christ,*
   to those who through *the righteousness of our God and Savior*
   Jesus Christ have received *a faith as precious as ours:"*

1) Here is our first "through." Our faith is a gift, given us *through* the character of Jesus; His righteousness is the source. This points us away from ourselves and anything we could do. Our responsibility is to use and develop this faith, as Peter will explain.

2) It is of *"our God and Savior Jesus Christ."* This is a clear statement of Christ's divinity, of His being both God and Savior. A great point to use in witnessing. It is echoed in verse 11 with exactly the same grammar: *"our Lord and Savior Jesus Christ."* Very few would disagree with that second statement, so they must accept the first one of Christ being both God and Savior.

3) Note the clarity of the statement *"have received,"* --we have faith, it has been given. This is a certainty we can rest in, take up and use.

2 Peter 1:2 *"Grace and peace be yours in abundance"*
God wants to give to us lavishly, fully, richly, bounteously. We need to live in that richness of His grace and peace!

"through the knowledge *of God and of Jesus our Lord."*

Here is our second "through." This grace and peace come to us *through* our knowledge of the Father and the Son. The more we know them and of them, the more grace and peace will flow into our lives. Therefore we need to be ever learning more and more about them through the Word, through obeying them and trusting them, so we may have grace and peace in growing abundance. Note here also that God and Jesus are presented as two separate persons, emphasizing the complex truth of the Trinity: one God, three Persons.

2 Peter 1:3 *"His divine power"*

This refers to Jesus our Lord, another direct statement of His divinity.

"has given us everything *we need for life and godliness"*

Wow! We already have *everything* we need to live for Him! We can never say it's impossible to resist temptation even though we may feel that way. Instead we need to learn to take up His provision and use it. This highlights the fact that we mistakenly often spend time praying for things He's already given us, like patience. Our prayers instead should be for help to skillfully take up and use all He's provided—which Peter will delineate further down in the text.

"through our knowledge *of him who called us by his own glory and goodness."*

Here's the third "through" and again it refers to knowledge of Christ. It is in knowing Him that all flows into our lives. We need to know Him in every dimension of our lives, specifically the seven areas we will look at. Are we learning more of Him, seeking to learn more daily? He is to be the center of our affection and attention in life.

2 Peter 1:4 "Through *these"*

21

Our fourth "through," this time referring to Christ's glory and goodness, the source from which He has blessed us with life, light and love. Because He is very glorious and totally good, we can trust Him.

"he has given us *his very great and precious promises,"*

These *have been* given and are to be received. And these promises are many, such as, *"...surely I am with you always, to the very end of the age"* (Matt. 28:20). We need to note, learn and think the truth of these promises, which also include the coming list of seven items we are to take up and use.

"so that through them *"*

The fifth "through." This time through His wonderful promises, the doorways to great things, such as, *"...to all who received him, to those who believed in his name, he gave the right to become children of God* (John 1:12).

"you may participate in the divine nature"

Another, bigger "Wow!" statement—we may taste and partake of *the* divine nature as we believe and receive the Holy Spirit! We have the nature of God, of Christ within us! The indwelling of the Holy Spirit--the same One Moses, David and Isaiah had! The same Spirit that indwelt Christ! What a gift! Christ is thereby always with us.

"and escape the corruption in the world caused by evil desires."

A further "Wow!" We don't have to remain captive to our sin, but can escape that corruption, being given a new nature that is able to escape/overcome our evil desires as we learn to avail ourselves of the help He has given, as Peter will explain. But this is only a reality when we lead ourselves well in following Peter's direction, which he now gives.

2 Peter 1:5 *"For this very reason, make* every effort *"*

The preceding verses give the "why" to obedience, delineating all that God has given and entrusted to us. Now comes

22

the "how." God has provided all we need to live a godly life. Our response should be to make every effort to eagerly, wholeheartedly, enthusiastically take up this provision and live well for Him. Following is the list of what He's provided. Note that these come in a specific order; we cannot pick and choose the order or the items.

"make every effort to add to your faith virtue;"

Faith is the gift given; now we should take up virtue, another gift. This word, also translated "goodness," has the idea of agreeing with God. If He says, "No!" then I whole-heartedly agree, running away from what is wrong. If He says, "Yes!" then I obey, whole-heartedly and immediately.
Virtue here is submitting my intellect to God's Word: He knows better than I do in every area. We can do submit and obey because God is good, almighty, wise, merciful, just and faithful. Our surrender is an act of trusting in His character.

"Make every effort to add...to virtue, knowledge;"

After the commitment to obey comes the delving into His Word to find out how to obey Him: reading, studying, memorizing, personalizing and praying it. As we saw above, many things come to us through our knowledge of God, so it is no surprise that knowledge comes second in the line. This study of His Word should be a very high priority in our lives.

2 Peter 1:6 *"Make every effort to add...to knowledge, self-control;"*

Once we've learned what God wants, then we need to act on this knowledge. And God gives us the will and strength to be self-controlled through His divine power, which flows to us through our knowledge of Him. It is our surrender (adding goodness) and what we learn of His Word (adding knowledge) that opens the way to add self-control.
It is important to note that we are not to work up self-control, but to take it up as what God has provided for us in our "tool-box" of standard equipment. Our job is to "add" it, knowing that God is providing. We will talk more about this later in the book.

"Make every effort to add...to self-control, perseverance;"

Here is where most of us fall down. We obey, but when

23

things get harder, or don't work out, we tend to revert to our natural responses, retreating to some comfortable place rather than pressing on in difficult obedience. We tend to follow our emotions, not truth.

This stage of perseverance is a reminder of our weakness and our need for Him and His power in our lives. It is also the opportunity to go on by faith rather than by sight. Will we pass the test? Will we press on and triumph with Him or will we give up, opting for comfort instead? Will we be more than conquerors or just cope? It is very important that we do persist, for we cannot go to the next stage if we don't.

"Make every effort to add...to perseverance, godliness;"

This word, "godliness" has the idea of looking to God, looking at God and being transformed into His likeness. As it says in 2 Corinthians 3:18 ESV, *"And we all, with unveiled face, beholding the glory of the Lord, are being transformed into the same image from one degree of glory to another. For this comes from the Lord who is the Spirit."*

As we persevere in doing what is right in the face of difficulty, we are encouraged, often forced to look to God for help, to find comfort, courage and guidance in His Word, to gaze on His beauty in worship and so are transformed by the Spirit. We become godly because of His glory. And this comes from persevering through difficulty

"Make every effort to add...to godliness, brotherly kindness;"

With this transformation comes the ability to love those prickly, unattractive, difficult fellow believers, to love them as God loves us. As we grow in our knowledge of God, we will also grow in our understanding of the depravity of our own flesh (old man)— we too are prickly, unattractive and difficult in our old nature. When we, like Paul, know that we are the "chief of sinners" we can much more easily forgive and love others as we have been undeservedly loved and forgiven by God.

"Make every effort to add...to brotherly kindness, love."

This moves us on to the agape love of God where we can let His unconditional love flow through us to the world by looking at people and things with His eyes. As we know how much He's loved us when we don't deserve it, we can then love others who don't

24

deserve it—which includes all people.

So, How important is it to God that we take up and use these gifts of His? Peter goes on to tell us:

"For if you possess these qualities in increasing measure, *they will keep you* from being ineffective and unproductive in your knowledge *of our Lord Jesus Christ."*

Did you catch that? Without these qualities, which He has freely provided for our use, we will be useless for God: ineffective and unproductive. But with them we will be productive and effective, pleasing and glorifying to God. This is where the title of this book comes from: EFFECTIVE. God's promise of effectiveness is tied to our leading ourselves well by adding these qualities in increasing measure.

Pretty straightforward: this is important to God! Very Important! This is the way He has laid out for us to be profitable sons and daughters in His Kingdom. So this should be very important to us because we live to love God. The next verse gives us the opposite side.

"But if anyone does not have them, [these seven qualities we are supposed to add] *he is nearsighted and blind, and has forgotten that he has been cleansed from his past sins."*

Failure to take up and use these gifts results in being a hindrance to God's plans. Note that the key result of failing to add these qualities is not knowing our own depravity. If we forget what we've been cleansed from, we tend to be proud, self sufficient, judgmental of others and abhorrent to God.

"Therefore, my brothers, be all the more eager to make your calling and election sure."

Knowing these truths should make us very eager to join God in what He's doing. To obey in these areas brings out the reality of our new life, our new nature, our new relationship with God. To obey in adding these qualities to our faith makes our calling by God to join Him in His great plan more sure, powerful and obvious.

"For if you do these things, you will never fall,"

25

There's another "Wow!" statement. Guaranteed success! If we are continually taking up and using these qualities, growing in these areas, we will never fall! This is Effectiveness with a capital E! Who wouldn't want such success and to finish well as the next verse says.

"and you will receive a rich welcome into the eternal kingdom of our Lord and Savior Jesus Christ."

To hear, "well done my good and faithful servant," to enter into the joy of the Lord--these are great motivations for obedience to Him now so that we will bring Him more and more glory throughout our lives, culminating in the pleasure we will give Him and receive from Him when we enter Heaven.

As we go through the next chapers, you will see how these seven items dovetail well with the seven categories we will consider.

Chapter 4   What's a Worldview Got To Do With It?

It has been said, "God is most glorified in us when we are most satisfied in Him."[4] This statement is in strong conflict with our western worldview, which tells us that satisfaction comes from self-fulfillment, self-centered comfort and self-focused pleasure, not from God. We are called on daily to choose between these two worldviews: that of our culture and that of the Bible.

A worldview is the system by which we try to make sense of the environment around us. Each culture has a general worldview that members unconsciously absorb. Then we each develop a personal worldview within our cultural one, drawing on input from our family, religion, education, environment and personal choices.

The single most important aspect of any cultural or personal worldview is our understanding of God, for this then determines the highest values we will live by.

Think about the differences between the worldviews of an atheist, a militant Jihadist and a conservative follower of Jesus. The atheist acts as his own god, deciding what is right and wrong, often living a self-centered existence. His highest value is to please himself.

The militant jihadist is willing to kill unsuspecting, uninvolved victims in order to advance the cause of his religion, thinking that this pleases his god and brings the jihadist honor; and gaining personal honor is his highest value.

The follower of Jesus seeks to be a carrier of light and life, loving those around him and sharing his faith with any who want to hear. He is willing to die for his faith, not kill for it. He can offer the sacrifice of thanksgiving in the most difficult of circumstances because he knows that the Lord Jesus is powerful, wise, good and loving; he knows that Jesus has a plan and is working it out no matter what. His highest value is to give honor to his God, which results in positive, edifying living.

The differences among these worldviews are immense and they stem entirely from the God/god each serves.

Volitional Worldview Shifts in the Pages of Scripture

When we are convicted that our cultural worldview is, at

---

[4] Title of a Piper sermon on Christian Hedonism. Listen to it at http://www.desiringgod.org/resource-library/sermons/god-is-most-glorified-in-us-when-we-are-most-satisfied-in-him

some point, in conflict with God's biblical worldview, we have the opportunity to switch to God's side. Making such a switch is what I call a *volitional worldview shift.*

There are a multitude of examples of volitional worldview shifts in the Bible, each one flowing from an individual getting a larger grasp of God's greatness.

- o Abraham going from protecting himself by hiding behind his wife in Egypt, to being willing to sacrifice his son Isaac.
- o Joseph going from being a whiner in the pit to being God's spokesman to Pharaoh and leader of a nation.
- o Moses going from being afraid to speak up to being willing to face Pharaoh and deliver God's people.
- o David going from being a plotter of adultery and murderer to a repentant sinner in response to Nathan's rebuke.
- o Isaiah being willing to volunteer for a difficult, fruitless ministry after seeing of the glory of God.
- o Peter realizing his sin and unworthiness when he saw Jesus' power for the first time in the great catch of fish.
- o Paul going from being a persistent persecutor of the church to a passionate proclaimer of the gospel as he saw the glory of Christ on the way to Damascus.

The author of Psalm 119 in verse 34 asks God for a worldview shift and then states the powerful results of that: *"Give me understanding,* [seeing things from God's view] *and I will keep your law and obey it with all my heart."* When we have God's understanding, we have His view, His worldview. This results in a significant shift in our values and commitments, moving us from obeying out of duty to obeying "with all my heart."

Then in 119:66 is another statement of a worldview shift: *"Teach me knowledge and good judgment, for I believe in your commands."* Here is a worldview shift from his own experience and judgment to a submission of the author's intellect to God's Word. We often unknowingly believe only certain parts of the Bible, the parts that are comfortable for us (such as, "to those who believed he gave the right to become the children of God" John 1:), but are reluctant to believe the parts that clash with our personal preferences (such as, "if your brother sins against you go and talk to him").

Worldview shifts are not limited to a certain select few. God is ever at work to bring such shifts to all His children, to move us from our limited, legalistic souls to the wide green pastures of wisdom He has for us. Jesus was ever at work in his earthly ministry to bring worldview shifts in all his followers.

Worldview Clash: Eternal Life Versus This Life's Riches

In Luke 18:18-27 we are told about Jesus' encounter with the rich young ruler and then with His disciples as He seeks to lead them in worldview shifts.

"A certain ruler asked him, 'Good teacher, what must I do to inherit eternal life?'" As we will see, this man is looking for the minimum he can do to get into Heaven; no whole-hearted following of God for him.

"'Why do you call me good?' Jesus answered. 'No one is good—except God alone.'" Here is Jesus' first challenge to the ruler's worldview, one which says that people are basically good and the young ruler certainly sees himself as good. Jesus rejects this view and points to the only truly good One. He may have also been calling the young man to recognize Him as God as well.

"'You know the commandments: Do not commit adultery, do not murder, do not steal, do not give false testimony, honor your father and mother.'" Jesus points him to the unattainably high standards of the law which no one has ever been able to keep.

"'All these I have kept since I was a boy,' he said." Who is he kidding? Is he saying that he always honored his mother and father every minute? Did he never lie, never look in lust at a woman? Certainly he did all these and much more. But he is blinded to his sin by his low view of God's holiness, which then determines his faulty worldview, including a highly unrealistic perception of himself as a good law keeper.

Jesus notes this and challenges him on the point where his false standard will be most clearly exposed. In doing this, Jesus illustrates that an opportunity for a worldview shift will always entail both a new view of God's greatness and a deeper exposure of our innate depravity.

"When Jesus heard this, he said to him, 'You still lack one thing. Sell everything you have and give to the poor, and you will have treasure in heaven. Then come, follow me.'

"When he heard this, he became very sad, because he was a man of great wealth."

This man was unwilling to give up his wealth for eternal life. He was looking for an easy way to get into Heaven while keeping all he had for himself. What Jesus demanded was too much: it was a call to trust God rather than his riches for his security and future. In the young ruler's worldview, comfort and security in the present outweighed the infinite future benefits of eternal life. His view of God was a minimal one where God was not able to take care of him. He refused to make a worldview shift.

After the young ruler leaves, the focus shifts to the disciples. *"Jesus...said, 'How hard it is for the rich to enter the kingdom of God! It is easier for a camel to go through the eye of a needle than for a rich man to enter the kingdom of God.'"*
Here Jesus is challenging his other listeners' worldview: they believed that since the wealthy had the time and resources to keep the law they had a greater possibility of being saved through it.
"Those who heard this asked, 'Who then can be saved?'"
This answer showed that Jesus had successfully put a crack in their worldview: works won't do it, no matter how much you try—but they didn't yet understand that faith was the means of salvation.
"Jesus replied, 'What is impossible with men is possible with God.'" In conclusion Jesus points them to God; only He can do the saving because men cannot. And eventually, at least His disciples made the shift to a biblical worldview of salvation by faith.

Types of Worldview Shifts

Our worldview locks us into a certain perspective. No fundamental changes can be made in our lives without a shift in our worldview. For instance, up through the 8th grade, my younger son was a poor student. He was basically lazy, doing just enough to get by. His highest values were being comfortable and cool, and he was busy pleasing himself. He was emotionally a functional atheist, setting his own standards, following his own values.
Then in his first year of high school he joined the cross-country team and found that he had a lot of running talent. He began to work hard at his sport, finding more and more success and enjoying it.
Then it clicked with him: working hard for any good thing is worthwhile. Here was a worldview shift: his highest value changed from being as comfortable as possible to using his abilities well. Then this worldview shift spilled over from running into other areas of his life as he began to work at his studies, at his friendships and then in his spiritual life. In the spiritual area he later made the

switch from living for himself to living for Jesus, which brought a cascade of positive changes.

Leading ourselves well has to do with making such "volitional worldview shifts," as opposed to "crisis-induced worldview shifts." Let me explain the difference.

A crisis-induced worldview shift comes from new understanding being forced on us by circumstances. A friend of ours who was 30 or 40 pounds overweight most of his life was diagnosed in his mid 50s with diabetes. Shocked by this development--he knew about the cascade of accompanying physical problems that can flow from being diabetic--he immediately began to work at losing weight, shedding those extra pounds over the next year.

He now looks great, his symptoms of diabetes are gone and he said he feels wonderful. The news of his becoming diabetic brought about a crisis-induced worldview shift from one of self-indulgence to one of self-discipline in order to avoid further medical problems.

In contrast, a volitional worldview shift is when God gives us insight through His Word or through seeing the application of His Word in our lives and we then choose to join Him by rejecting our natural worldview at this point and adopting His.

Examples of Volitional Worldview Shifts

A few years back I was meditating on Psalm 34.[5] Having memorized this passage, I was praying through it and the Spirit opened my eyes to a deeper, wider, more powerful view of God and His majestic and mighty Character.

In the opening verses David displays his passion for exalting God: six times in three verses he declares his intention to praise God in every circumstance. Listen to his intensity as he calls us to join him in his worldview shift.

"I will extol the LORD at all times;
his praise will always be on my lips.
My soul will boast in the LORD;
let the afflicted hear and rejoice.
Glorify the LORD with me;
let us exalt his name together" (Ps. 34:1-3).

This desire to praise God was ignited as David saw God's

---

[5] See appendix A for an explanation of mediation on Scripture as I am using it here.

faithfulness and power in protecting him from the Philistine king, Abimelech. David experienced God's deliverance both internally and externally and, knowing Scripture well, saw in a greater way the faithfulness of God, which he then wrote about in Psalm 34. Listen again to the excitement in David's voice as he describes this new revelation of God's faithfulness, power and precision in answering.

"I sought the LORD, and he answered me;
he delivered me from all my fears. [internal deliverance]
Those who look to him are radiant;
their faces are never covered with shame. [evidence of internal deliverance]
This poor man called, and the LORD heard him;
he saved him out of all his troubles" [external deliverance] (Ps. 34:4-6).

David goes on to give the reason for his worldview shift to greater trust in God and a desire to focus on worship; in this he makes clear statements of God's persistent provision at all times.

"The angel of the LORD encamps around those who fear him, and
he delivers them.
Taste and see that the LORD is good;
blessed is the man who takes refuge in him" (Ps. 34:7,8).

David had just experienced this deliverance and protection in God's refuge. Now he calls us to walk with him in fearing and trusting the mighty God who takes care of His servants

Fear the LORD, you his saints,
for those who fear him lack nothing.
The lions may grow weak and hungry,
but those who seek the LORD lack no good thing" (Ps. 34:9,10).

I was deeply moved by these insights and was also convicted of the shallowness of my trust in God, evidenced by the complaining, grumbling, impatience and fear in my life. The contrast of my own life with those opening verses was stark. With the Spirit's help I chose to move with David into a life of praise.

First came confession and repentance of my lack of faith evidenced by complaining. Then I chose to shift my focus from my circumstances to the mighty and magnificent Shepherd who is leading me through them, protecting, guiding and giving me grace.

And thirdly, I committed to seeking to praise my powerful God in everything.

I knew this was going to be a learning process, but it couldn't start without a commitment. What followed was an uphill journey into greater freedom, growing joy and illumination of truth. There was also a deepening hope, increasing power and broader understanding of how God is at work. That upward spiral continues to today. It is wonderful!

Our gracious God is constantly working to lead us in making and living in such worldview shifts. If we don't pay attention to the Word and the Spirit, He will use other means to get our attention, as He did with the fellow with diabetes.

Think how much more glory that fellow could have given God if, in his early years as a believer, he'd acknowledged the sin of abusing the temple of God (his body) and had denied the push of his natural worldview to use his body primarily for pleasure, thereby disciplining himself for godliness by taking care of his body?

Well, I'm getting a bit ahead of myself here, but the excitement of seeing the grandeur and glory of our Lord's perfect and powerful character, the wonder of basking in the illumination of His Word and the joy of choosing to think His thoughts moves my whole being--mind, will and emotions--to want to share with you what He has in store for us.

In all this, God is calling us to a growing partnership with Him. He has prepared all: His Word, a plan for our growth, experiences to bring insight, and His Spirit to teach us. If we are not spending time with Him, delving deeply into His Word, opening our mind, will and emotions to the Spirit's instruction, we will have to settle not for 2nd best, but for the 5th best of "crisis worldview shifts."

So I call you to join me, in looking in the seven areas of life so we can join God in this adventure of growth, revelation and joy that He has prepared for us.

Chapter 5   What Does It Mean To Lead Yourself Well Spiritually?

"Make every effort to add to your faith, virtue…" 2 Peter 1:5

Leading yourself well spiritually begins, Peter tells us, with *"adding to your faith, virtue"* (2 Peter 1:5). This is to be done after having some worldview shifts that we touched on in chapter three. The first is grasping that Jesus, by *"His divine power has given us everything we need for life and godliness!" "Has given"* means that we already have available all we need. When I feel like I am lacking something to help me be godly, this verse gives me a sound basis of truth for rejecting that wrong impression.

The second is that *"…he has given us his very great and precious promises, so that through them you may participate in the divine nature and escape the corruption in the world caused by evil desires"* (2 Pet 1:3,4). We have very complete equipping! But equipment is nothing if we don't avail ourselves of it.

Having these two worldview shifts, we can now proceed to add to our faith this series of qualities, beginning with virtue.

This word, virtue or goodness, has the concept of agreeing with God. It is a surrender to Him and His values. If He says something is to be avoided, I run the other way. If He says I should do something, then without hesitation I obey. He is calling us to join Him in all He's doing.

It is like God hands us a blank contract and says, "Sign it and later I'll tell you the conditions." And because we know Him, we can trust Him in this: He will never ask us to do anything contrary to His character.

Leading myself well spiritually means foundationally to value God and His revelation of Himself above all other things in my life. He is to be the pinnacle, the purpose, the passion of my life.

Therefore, **the most important thing we can do** in leading ourselves well spiritually, I believe, is to **continually nurture our first love for Jesus.** All else will flow from that.

How Can I "Nurture My First Love?"

The full August moon was just above the horizon, shining brightly in the warm evening air. We walked hand in hand across the newly mown field, breathing in the intoxicating scent of drying hay. I glanced down at the lovely woman walking gracefully by my side, her soft hair shining in the moonlight. She looked up at me, her almond eyes gleaming. She smiled dreamily, and gently squeezed my hand.

My heart was full to overflowing with wonder and joy. That such a godly, exotic, beautiful woman could love me, want to be with me, consider spending her life with me—this was amazing, truly awesome. I was overwhelmed with the grandeur of the moment and the loveliness of what God was doing in our lives. I was attracted by her love for Jesus and was deeply, profoundly in love with this extraordinary woman!

Twenty years later on another August evening we sat in the moonlight on the balcony of our apartment in the Middle East. This time, however, instead of gazing at each other in love, we had turned our backs towards each other. We were not thinking about the moonlight or beauty or love. We had just had sharp words and I, at least, was thinking about my hurt. I was not in love; I was angry.

The Holy Spirit, however, was not sitting idly by. He began nudging me, reminding me of why I had married this strong woman. She loved Jesus passionately. She loved to pray. She had a heart for the lost. She knew the Scriptures well, had a quiet time every day and tried to live what she learned. She had followed me through more than a decade of hard life, doing church planting in a difficult, dangerous, closed country. She was a wise advisor, a wonderful cook and a good mother as well as beautiful in face and form.

As I thought on these facets of her rich and varied personality, my anger receded. The smallness of our disagreement was exposed, and the basis of our marriage--a love for Jesus and a desire to serve Him together--engulfed my negative thoughts. My first love was renewed. I was able to humble myself and ask for forgiveness for my part of our disagreement.

Nurturing our first love is focusing on and delighting in the other's qualities, remembering how we first came to love that one and rejoicing in the privilege of having a relationship with such a person.

So it is with Jesus: we can daily be renewing our first love by looking on His beautiful, awesome, powerful character, remembering our early days of new birth and the ways He has guided and protected us since then.

What Did He Have To Say About First Love?

The Lord Jesus Himself agrees that nurturing our first love

is the foundational discipline for a godly life. In His words to the church at Ephesus in Revelation 2, Jesus first commends them for nine different positives. He makes it sound like the church in Ephesus was healthy, strong and destined for a powerful, productive future.

Then He says this: *"Yet I hold this against you: You have forsaken your first love. Remember the height from which you have fallen! Repent and do the things you did at first"* (Rev. 2:4,5).

Two important points stand out here. First, if we don't intentionally nurture our first love, it will grow cold and we will forsake it, as the Ephesians did. Second, this forsaking of our first love is sin: Christ calls the Ephesians to repent! A strong first love leads you to being passionately committed to Jesus and obeying Him.

Jesus doesn't stop there, however. To emphasize the seriousness of nurturing our first love, Jesus adds, *"If you do not repent, I will come to you and remove your lampstand from its place"* (Rev. 2:6). In other words, failure to repent and return to a first love would result in an end to the church—and historically that is just what happened to the congregation in Ephesus: it was snuffed out by a lack of love for Christ.

A Biblical Example of Nurturing First Love

Asaph, the author of several Psalms, was passionate about his relationship with God; in one psalm he said to God, *"...earth has nothing I desire besides you"* (Ps. 73:25). But he did not come to this place of godly passion and focus without intentionally leading himself there. He had to work at nurturing his first love for God in the midst of intense opposition from his own heart.

As you may know, Asaph does not begin Psalm 73 with a focus on the spiritual. After a quick nod to God, he falls into a swamp of emotional turmoil, wrestling with complaining, jealousy and anger: *"...I envied the arrogant when I saw the prosperity of the wicked....Surely in vain have I kept my heart pure; in vain have I washed my hands in innocence"* (Ps. 73:3,13).

He was unable to extricate himself from this quicksand of complaining and anger, *"When I tried to understand all this, it was oppressive to me...."* (Ps. 73:16). Without the spiritual element in the picture, Asaph was trapped in a natural worldview, unable to throw off the bitter, negative thoughts of his heart. But—and here's the key--he did not stay there.

"...it was oppressive to me till I entered the sanctuary of

God; then I understood their [the wicked's] final destiny. Surely you place them on slippery ground; you cast them down to ruin" (Ps 73:16b-18).

He turned to God, he went to worship in the temple, and it was in worship, in focusing on the character of the great and wise Creator, that God gave him a perspective outside of human understanding. Asaph got a wider, longer view of life and how God was working. Only this worldview shift could free Asaph from his complaining, jealous and negative heart.

With this new supernatural perspective, looking down on the situation from God's wide vantage point, Asaph could see how badly he'd gone wrong: *"When my heart was grieved and my spirit embittered, I was senseless and ignorant; I was a brute beast before you"* (Ps. 73:21,22).

If we don't lead ourselves well spiritually, this is where we end up, operating in the ignorance of a human worldview, and even worse, thinking and acting like animals--just what Satan wants for us.

God also showed Asaph that even when he was in such a rebellious state that God had been there with him all along, loving, guiding and protecting him. Asaph declared, *"Yet I am always with you; you hold me by my right hand. You guide me with your counsel, and afterward you will take me into glory"* (Ps 73:23,24).

What a beautiful God we have! The Lord Jesus, our great Shepherd, never leaves us, even when we are bitter, senseless and rebellious. He's always there, always working to draw us back to Himself, to His love, to Truth, to freedom, to holiness.

In seeing God more clearly as his faithful, powerful and lovely Lord, Asaph's response was one of passion: *"Whom have I in heaven but you? And earth has nothing I desire besides you. My flesh and my heart may fail, but God is the strength of my heart and my portion forever"* (Ps. 73:25,26).

This was a volitional worldview shift on Asaph's part, based on his wider view of God. He rejected thinking as a mere human being where he operated only on what he could observe, reason and feel. He submitted his intellect, will and emotions to the Word and whole-heartedly switched to God's perspective. Why? Because of his new vision of what God is like: Just, Holy and Firm, punishing sin while being Forgiving, Faithful and Persistent, Powerful and Protecting.

Leading ourselves well spiritually means that even when we fall into failures, into sin and wrong thinking, we will, like Asaph, turn to God, lift our souls to Him[6], meditate on the glory and goodness of His being, and surrender. We will cooperate with God in having our negatives turned into spiritual advances by gazing on His beauty and holiness, by nurturing our first love for Him.

---

[6] For an explanation of lifting one's soul to God, see my book *EQUIPPED! pp. 151-168*

Chapter 6   What Can I Do to Nurture My First Love for Jesus?

What the Lord Jesus wants from us is a commitment to nurture our first love for Him every day. If we want to add to our faith virtue, then we will want to obey Him in this.

Nurturing our first love is not something to leave just for when things are difficult; we should be doing this daily, spending time in personal worship in our quiet times and reminding ourselves of what a wonderful Lord we have. It's so easy to forget in the rush of every day life, which is reason we need a worldview shift which leads to continually nurturing our first love.

The foundational question is, "how do we go about it?" Simply put, Asaph showed us the way: it starts with worship, goes on to confession, then the Word, then to surrender.

Note carefully: these are activities that can easily become legalistic practices. However, the focus of these activities is not the fulfilling of some program, it is not legalistically ticking off certain disciplines each day. No, the focus is on the Lord Jesus Himself, on getting to know Him better, loving Him more. It's relational, not legalistic, it's personal, not a program, it's internal, not external.

So how can you practically do this? There are a good number of ways, and here I share with you one--what I do in my quiet time to nurture my first love for Jesus.

I consistently include the following elements.
--Transforming worship
--Transparent confession
--Truth-transporting liturgy
--Total commitment reading
--Tenacious intercession.

Bear with me as I unpack each of these a bit for you.

Transforming Worship

This has to do with an intentional focus on the Character of Christ, the living God, praising Him for who He is, trying not to think about how He benefits me. He is worthy of my worship even if everything in my life is going wrong. To know Him is all I need for joy. My whole purpose in life is to love and worship Him.

Personally I take a Psalm each day, looking for the characteristics of God in it and use these as basis for praise. For instance, in Psalm 9:2 it says, *"I will be glad and rejoice in you; I will sing praise to your name, O Most High."*

In thinking on this verse, drawing from my knowledge of other Scripture, I wrote this in my worship journal, "Yes, Lord Jesus, you are the One worthy of worship. There is no one greater than you. You are the Most High: the Most High in wisdom, in power, in goodness, in love, in grace, in justice, in knowledge and in authority. You spoke and created the trillions of stars and millions of galaxies. You know each of them by name. At the same time you are the One who holds together the nucleus of every atom; you know the number of hairs on the head of every person and are at work bringing history to the conclusion you know is best. You are worthy of our awe, our admiration, obedience and worship. In you I rejoice and am glad!"

As I cultivate this kind of personal worship, I see more of His beauty, majesty and grandeur and my first love for Him deepens.

I find that writing out these words of worship is much more effective than just speaking or thinking them, for writing leads me to articulate thoughts more completely, to carry logic to its conclusion and to think in wider and deeper ways. Plus I then have something to share with others after I'm done.

If you would like more examples of such personal worship, look at appendix B. And if that is not enough, get a copy of the devotional book *EDIFIED!*[7] which will give you one year's worth of such worship.

Transparent Confession

As I worship, I stand in the light of Christ's beauty and purity; the Holy Spirit often uses this light to point out some of my sin: pride, selfishness, pettiness, unbelief, complaining, lust and self-sufficiency, to name a few.

I can choose to draw back into the shadows and cover these sins over, or I can step out more into the light and whole-heartedly embrace the reality of these, confessing them to God. He knows about them anyway, so why try to hide them?

Being transparent before Him also deepens my love for Him, for in confession I receive His forgiveness, experiencing afresh how He is *"Good, ready to forgive and abundant in mercy to*

---

[7] *EDIFIED! 365 Devotions to Stimulate Personal Worship and Spark Inner Transformation.* Available at www.edifyingservices.com

all who call on Him " (Ps. 86:5 NKJV). He delights in our confession and in being able to forgive us.

In addition, such transparent confession helps me to be honest with myself, and to marvel that Jesus can love me so when I still have my old nature, in which dwells no good thing (Rom. 7:18). As I see more of God's glory, and then more of my depravity, my wonder, joy and thankfulness for being His child grows—as does my first love for Him.

Truth-transporting Liturgy:

Each day I take at least one passage of Scripture, which I've memorized and use it as a prayer to God. It becomes my "liturgy" for a period of time. Ephesians 6:10-18 is my most used one, the putting on of the armor of God.[8] Another daily one is Ephesians 3:16-19, asking for power to know the Love of Christ better. And there are many more that we can use.

One way to begin using Scripture as prayer is to look for the prayers that Paul wrote into the Word and use them. Then you can go on to pick other passages that strike you. Personalizing and praying these passages transports their truths down into your soul, bringing deep, ongoing transformation to your mind, will and emotions as well as nurturing your first love.

Total Commitment Reading

Then comes regular reading through the Bible. I read at least a chapter in the NT each morning, and a chapter in the OT each evening. I read the Psalms separately, using them in my morning worship times. Reading this way takes me continuously through His Word, reminding me of the overview as well as the details.

As I read, I am committed to obey whatever the Spirit brings to my attention. I do not want to give myself the option to pick and choose what I apply. The Spirit is the One who brings out what I need to be doing in response to what I've read. My part is to obey.

Tenacious Intercession

Intercessory prayer is God's invitation for us to join Him in

---

[8] See Appendix C for an example of praying through Ephesians 6:10-18

41

what He is doing. Ignoring prayer means we are doing our own thing, not God's. It also is an indication of our arrogance: we think we can handle life on our own so don't seek God's gracious help.

Rejecting these two errors, I spend time every day interceding for a variety of people, events and activities. In addition to hearing and answering my prayers, the Spirit is interacting with me in these prayers, guiding and teaching me more about Himself, about me living for Him. Sometimes the Spirit points out that what I pray for another is just what I need to be doing myself! He shows me more of Christ, more of the world and it's needs, and more of the depth of God's Word as I pray it for others. I get nearer to the heart of Jesus.[9]

Making the Shift

Having such a basic quiet time isn't too hard to implement if you start small. You can begin with 3 minutes for worship, 2 minutes for confession, 5 minutes for reading and 3 minutes for truth transporting liturgy—that's 13 minutes. Then praying though the list of those you are responsible for spiritually is an added factor, which can be spread throughout the day. Start with 5 minutes of intercessory prayer.

However, the bottom line is that without a worldview shift here, it is unlikely that you would persist in nurturing your first love for Jesus like this. There is just too much competition in life for your time and affection. Here are the two elements of a volitional worldview shift that could result in your leading yourself well in this area.

A Changed View of God: Grasping that He is the Creator, the Sustainer and the Ender of all. He is so magnificently great, so awesomely good, so perfectly pure, so majestically powerful, so eternally sovereign, so lavishly loving that He is worthy of my wholehearted worship, my total devotion and my unconditional love. He is by far the most important One in my life. No one can come close, for He is utterly other than any part of creation. He is the center and pinnacle of my life.

A Volitional Worldview Shift: In adding to my faith virtue

---

[9] If you would like to read more about these aspects of a good, rich, powerful quiet time, you can find more in the book, *EQUIPPED! Ready for Everyday Spiritual Warfare.* available at: www.edifyingservices.com

(agreeing with God), I declare that my relationship with the Almighty God, the Lord Jesus, is the most important aspect of my whole existence. The most significant thing I can do is to spend time with Him every day, nurturing my first love for Jesus. It is the best, wisest and smartest investment of time. Nothing else can compare with it. The Creator of the universe is there, waiting for me each morning when I wake up, wanting to spend time with me! What more could I ask for?!!! So I *will* meet with Him every day—no matter what the obstacle! This comes first, always, no matter what. Nothing will deter me from meeting with my loving God!

Two Warnings.

First, no worldview shift comes without a challenge to it by the world, our flesh and the Devil. Expect it. When the competition comes (when you are too tired, too busy, too distracted, too tempted by the tinsel of this world), then you need to look away again to our great and marvelous God, looming far over all creation, unsurpassable in beauty, goodness, power, wisdom and grace. Why wouldn't I want to meet with Him?!

Second, the element of time in relation to meeting with God is not central. My quiet time is not predicated on an amount of time, but upon the five aspects listed above (worship, confession, liturgy, the Word and intercession).

If I am in a tightly scheduled situation (like being at a demanding conference), my quiet time may be 25 minutes long. Each element will be there, but short. Since I normally have a substantial quiet time each day, having a shorter one for a day or several days is fine. But I wouldn't want to subsist on such a meager meeting with God on a regular basis.

On a normal day, I do not look at the time at all, but at what I am doing with Jesus. I make time for each element, even if they have to be scattered throughout the day. No matter what, I am committed to meeting with Jesus, learning more of His wonderful Being, adding virtue to the faith He's given me.

Summary:

Lead yourself well

Spiritually: add to your faith, virtue by:

Nurturing your first love for Jesus.

"...if you possess these qualities in increasing measure, they will keep you from being ineffective and unproductive in your knowledge of our Lord Jesus Christ" (2 Pet. 1:8)

Action Plan:
If you have a quiet time, commit to continuing it every day, and make sure it includes worship (see Appendix B for examples).

If you don't have a regular quiet time, begin having one. Start with a 18 minute goal; if you do this, you will find yourself expanding this delightful time as you enjoy your time with Jesus.

> --5 minutes of reading (read a chapter a day, starting in Matthew and reading on through the whole NT).
> --3 minutes of worship (use a Psalm like 34, or look at Appendix B).
> --2 minutes of confession (ask the Spirit to point out anything you should confess to Him).
> --3 minutes of truth transporting liturgy (praying a passage).
> --5 minutes of prayer (for yourself, your family, friends, church, persecuted Christians and those who have never heard). Make a commitment to yourself and God to do this each day. Everyone has 18 minutes to spare. And everyone does what they really want to do.

Chapter 7   What Does It Mean To Lead Yourself Well Intellectually?

"Make every effort to...add to virtue, knowledge..." 2 Peter 1:5b

"Well, Bob, it's good to hear from you!" said Pastor John. "How long has it been now? Is it already four years since you left for the mission field? It seems like yesterday!"

"It's actually been four and a half," replied Bob. "And it didn't go by quite so quickly for me, what with language study and learning to fit into a new culture. But God gave grace and we were able to more than make it through. Now we're back here in the States and working on the schedule for our furlough. I'm going to be out there in California in March and wondered if we could set up a date to speak in your church in L.A.?"

"Oh, you didn't know!" replied Pastor John. "I've left that church and started another one in Bakersfield."
"Really?" said Bob. "No, I didn't know about that. Sounds good—
    doing church planting. Tell me about it."

"Well, it started with my divorce. That old church was just too narrow minded to understand the way God was working in my life, so we parted ways."

"Your divorce? You mean Robin left you?"

"No, actually, I left Robin. You see, as I grew in my understanding of God, I realized that one of His greatest desires is for us to be happy. And well, to be honest, Robin wasn't making me happy, so I found someone who would. And now we are married-- very happily I must add-- and have this new and thriving ministry."
"Really?!!!!"
"Yes. Would you like to come and speak in my new church?"
"Ahhhh….."

So how is pastor John doing in leading himself well intellectually? How biblical is his thinking? Where does he get his input from? Anyone who knows Scripture at all understands that God's primary desire for us is our being conformed to the image of Christ. He desires our maturity, godliness and obedience, which often are developed by going through difficulties (James 1:2-4). Joy, which is much deeper and richer than happiness, is then one side effect of knowing Jesus and obeying His Truth (John 15:11). However, if happiness is our goal, that has become an idol; it will be

45

ever illusive, for it is dependent on circumstances, which can easily change. Joy, however, is dependent on the character of God, which never changes; and joy can be there in the midst of the most difficult of circumstances

Pastor John has pretty obviously not been leading himself well intellectually; he's allowed himself to be led by his culture, not the truth of God's Word.

What's the Most Important Aspect?

God created us as whole beings, making us a pair of trinities: first spirit, soul and body; and then our soul being our mind, will and emotions. He wants every part of us involved in our relationship with Him and the mind is second in line after our spirit. Leading ourselves well intellectually is important to God and therefore to us.

This means first and foremost, I believe, learning to think like God, to think His thoughts rather than our own innate ones. We all have natural ways of thinking that flow from our own corrupted nature ("flesh" in biblical terms), where even the most altruistic thoughts are tainted with the soot of selfishness. For instance, I want to do good. But the important question is, "Why do I want this?"

> - Because, well, it makes me feel good;
> - So I can be fulfilled;
> - So others will do good to me;
> - So people will like me;
> - So people will think I'm a fine person;
> - So others won't do bad things to me;
> - So God will accept me, love me more, do more good to me.

Every one of these motives is self-centered, so the good we do is cancelled by our sin of selfishness. This is the result of following our hearts instead of the Word! In contrast, biblically we are called to follow Jesus and think like Him, to get into His Word, to absorb it, internalize it, live it. What were His motives in doing good?

> - To honor His Father
> - To proclaim the good news
> - To demonstrate the power and love of God
> - To meet the needs of people
> - To open hearts to repentance

Every one of these motives is God-directed, other directed.

This raises the level of good out of being sin-tainted to being sacrificial service to the glory of God. Jesus led Himself well intellectually because He was thinking the thoughts of His Father.

Leading ourselves well intellectually actually flows right out of leading ourselves well spiritually. As we cultivate our first love for Jesus, we will see more and more of His beauty, His holiness, His grace and goodness. We will learn that we can trust Him and His Word and we will desire to be like Him, to think like Him, asking ourselves the question, "What would He do in my situation?" We can only answer that question if we learn to think like Him.

The How of It

We must begin by accepting the fact that we cannot think like God unless He reveals His thoughts to us first. He says, " '...*my thoughts are not your thoughts, neither are your ways my ways,' declares the LORD. 'As the heavens are higher than the earth, so are my ways higher than your ways and my thoughts than your thoughts'*" (Isa. 55:8,9).

So we turn to His Revelation of Himself--His living, powerful Word, through which we can think like Him, see things as He sees them and therefore respond as He does.

As 2 Peter 1 says, this means adding to our virtue--our commitment of obedience--the knowledge of what God thinks and desires. So we commit ourselves to reading, studying, and most importantly, to meditating on the Bible.

First reading: It is very helpful to have some plan for reading the Bible. As mentioned in the last chapter, personally I read through the Bible constantly, taking one chapter of the NT each morning and at least one chapter of the OT in the evening. The Psalms I read separately as a basis for worship. At this rate, every two years I read the NT about 3 times and the OT once. Such continual reading gives me the needed overview as well as a review of the details. There are a myriad of other ways to read through the Bible. Find one that suits you and follow through.

Second, studying: I do this in preparation for lessons, for finding answers to my own questions, for following up on truths that stood out to me in my daily reading. This includes word studies and comparing Scripture and translations.

Third, meditation: This is by far the most powerful practice of all, one that results in really internalizing God's thoughts.

Meditation, as I am using it, means first memorizing Scripture; this brings transformation to our intellect by having God's Word and words literally in our minds. We can then think like Him. Second comes personalizing it, which brings transformation of our emotions. And third is praying the passage to be true in my life; this brings transformation of our will.

Please look at Appendix A for a more complete explanation of this type of meditation, including tips on how to persist in it.

Taking the time for such meditation leads us upward into new insights, new understanding and new aspects of the multilayered richness of the Word of God, revealing more and more of God's character and thought.

You have probably experienced the great value of memorizing passages of Scripture. Meditation then takes us two steps further (personalizing and praying the passage), resulting in inner transformation. This practice has been the greatest source of growth and learning in my life. I recommend it highly.

If we have meditated on God's Word, in a time of need the Holy Spirit can bring these verses to mind to give us direction, encouragement and warning. If, however, we have only a general knowledge of the Word, then the Holy Spirit doesn't have much to work with. And without the measure of the Word, we are adrift in an intellectual flood of input that can easily sweep us off into error.

Full Equipping

The combination of having the overview of Scripture from constant reading through it, along with the depth of memorized and meditated passages helps us to be aware of any error that comes into our lives. With this help we can lead ourselves well intellectually, selecting what is good and rejecting what is faulty in a conversation, a book, a speech, a discussion or a sermon. This is not just a matter of opinion; we can and must measure these things according to God's Word, the Bible.

One of the greatest needs in the church today is to discern where we are following culture instead of God—and we can only do this as we know the Word well. For instance, we can see where "worship" often becomes a means of entertainment instead of a means to focus us on God so we can forget ourselves and give Him honor.

To give this kind of priority to thinking like God requires

submitting our intellect to His Word. This is not hard as we get a growing grasp of God's greatness, which leads us to a volitional worldview shift.

Changed View of God: Our Triune Lord is the ultimate in intelligence. He is wiser than anyone else; His knowledge is greater, deeper, wider and longer than anyone else's. In comparison, mine is minimal, miniscule, microscopic! He knows the name of every star (all umpteen trillion of them), He understands all there is to know about atomic physics (He made it up). He is outside of time and knows all that will come in the future. He is the Beginner and Ender of history. He has a plan and will work it out no matter what people may do. He is the One we can trust, who shares with us in His Word all we need to know and will protect us from error through it.

Volitional Worldview Shift: Since God is so wise and knowledgeable, knowing God's Word intimately is THE most important goal I can have in my relationship with Him. Learning His Word is the most important initial response I can have to His love. Therefore I will commit myself to reading it daily, studying it regularly and memorizing it consistently so I can think His thoughts. To spend this time in these activities is the best investment I can make of all my resources.

Summary

Lead yourself well

Spiritually: add to your faith, virtue by
    Nurturing your first love for Jesus.
Intellectually: add to your virtue, knowledge by
    Learning to think God's thoughts through meditating on His Word.

"...if you possess these qualities in increasing measure, they will keep you from being ineffective and unproductive in your knowledge of our Lord Jesus Christ" (2 Pet. 1:8)

Action Plan:
    Before going on to the next chapter, take a few minutes to begin memorizing 1 Peter 1:5-7:

make every effort to add to your faith goodness; and to goodness,
    knowledge;
and to knowledge, self-control; and to self-control, perseverance;
    and to perseverance, godliness;
and to godliness, brotherly kindness; and to brotherly kindness,
    love.

Continue to work on this in your quiet time (2 minutes). Then when you have it memorized, pray it each day for yourself each day for at least a week. Here's an example of personalizing and praying it:

--Help me, Lord, to make every effort to add to my faith, virtue, agreeing with you on what is right and wrong.
--Help me to add to my virtue, knowledge. Help me to read your Word each day, and to work on memorizing it so you can use it to transform my thinking.
--Help me to add to my knowledge, self-control, to obey what I've learned in reading your Word. Help me not to fall into the trap of thinking that knowing something is enough, and instead do what I have learned.
--Help me to add to my self-control, endurance, pressing on through the difficulties that come, knowing that you are with me and helping in all.
--Help me to add to my endurance, godliness. May I look to you every day in worship and prayer, relying on you to help me endure.
--Help me to add to my godliness, brotherly kindness, being gracious to others as you are to me.
--Help me to add to my brotherly kindness, agape love, caring for all around me as you care for me.
Help me to see when I am straying from these points and to immediately repent and follow you. Amen.

Chapter 8   What Does It Mean To Lead Yourself Well Volitionally?

"Make every effort to...add to knowledge, self control...." 2 Peter 1:6.

After grabbing one last item, John ran back to the checkout line at Home Depot where his helper was waiting with all their purchases.

"Ok," said the cashier, "I've rung up all your items, so you can swipe your card now."

John looked at the total displayed on the card machine and blinked in surprise. "This is too low," he said to his friend.

"Shhhh. Don't say anything," whispered the helper.

"No, no, the cashier missed something." John replied, then paused. Turning directly to his friend he said, "You know, at the end of my life when I stand before God, He's going to ask me about this night at Home Depot and what I did. I want to do what will please Him so He will commend me, not condemn me. No, we'll pay for all we've gotten here."

Turning to the cashier John said, "I don't think you got everything. How about these FRP boards?"

"Oh, I didn't see those," she said, scanning in another $200 onto the bill.

Our will, or volition, is intended to be the center of the decision making process. We normally first get input from other sources such as spiritual, intellectual and emotional ones as well as friends and culture. Then, after evaluating these, we make a decision, hopefully with the Holy Spirit's help.

Without good input it is impossible to make a wise decision. And without having a self-controlled will, trained to respond to the input of virtue and knowledge, we are going to get ourselves into trouble.

In the above incident at Home Depot, John was using spiritual and intellectual input to decide that getting an illegitimate discount on his purchase was not the right choice. Having the big picture of time and eternity, he immediately saw it was not worth it.

However his friend, not having led himself well in spiritual and intellectual areas, was unprepared to make a wise decision when presented with the temptation to cheat, even though he was not the one paying the bill or reaping the benefit!

You can begin to see here the multiplying cascade of good that comes from leading ourselves well from the top as we make the needed worldview shifts. When we do this in the spiritual area (virtue) and in the intellectual area (biblical knowledge) it will definitely influence our decisions positively. Our commitment to obedience and our growing knowledge of God's Word and His ways can feed the proper input into our will so the decisions we make will be good, wise and pleasing to Him.

If you think about this, you can see that we have many opportunities each day to lead ourselves well volitionally. Do I barge through the door, or do I let the little old lady go through first? Do I run the red light since no one is coming or watching, or do I wait, looking at the empty street before me? Do I turn away from the sexually explicit ad or take a second look? Do I tell a little lie to make someone feel better, or do I ask for wisdom and give edifying advice? There are lots of chances every day to practice leading ourselves well volitionally.

The Number One Practice

So, what is the most important way to lead myself well volitionally? I believe it is by choosing to willfully, in faith, give thanks to God in and for everything.

You are familiar with verses that command us to do this, like 1 Thessalonians 5:18, *"...give thanks in all circumstances, for this is God's will for you in Christ Jesus."* My favorite verse on this subject, however, is the one that led me to another volitional worldview shift in this area.

Psalm 50:23 says, *"He who sacrifices thank offerings honors me, and he prepares the way so that I may show him the salvation of God."* Note that it does not say we should be thankful, which is an emotion, but to give an offering of thanks, which is an act of the will. This I can do no matter how I feel.

Notice also that this verse casts the giving of thanks as a sacrifice, that is, something that costs me, something which is difficult. It's a simple fact that there are many happenings in my life that I don't like and it is unnatural to give thanks for them; in fact it can be painful to do so. But God understands that and gives us three reasons for acting supernaturally here in offering the sacrifice of thanksgiving.

First, when we give thanks for difficult things, we are exercising faith, trusting our sovereign God to be at work protecting and guiding and gracing in this situation. To act in faith brings honor to Him and pleases Him.

In contrast, when we thank Him after getting an answer to prayer, there is no faith involved because we already have the answer. It is certainly good and right to thank Him for the answers, but it gives Him much more honor when we thank Him, in faith, before anything is worked out.

Second, is the truth that in giving thanks, we *"... prepare the way...."* That is, as we give thanks when we don't feel like it, we are joining God in what He is doing. We are laying the groundwork for Him to move into the situation to bring the needed help. We are opening the door for God to act.

Third, *"...that I may show him the salvation of God."* God is going to respond as we express our faith and cooperate with Him in giving thanks. He wants us to join Him in what He's doing. Giving thanks opens the way to God's help. Failure to give thanks-- that is complaining--keeps the door closed, blocking what God wants to do.

Two Examples

As a negative illustration of this, think of King Saul in 1 Samuel 13, reacting out of fear rather than trusting God.

"What have you done?" asked Samuel.

Saul replied, "When I saw that the men were scattering, and that you did not come at the set time, and that the Philistines were assembling at Micmash, I thought, 'Now the Philistines will come down against me at Gilgal, and I have not sought the LORD's favor.' So I felt compelled to offer the burnt offering." [Notice, Saul was acting on feeling, not truth.]

"You acted foolishly," Samuel said. "You have not kept the command the LORD your God gave you; if you had, he would have established your kingdom over Israel for all time. But now your kingdom will not endure; the LORD has sought out a man after his own heart and appointed him leader of his people, because you have not kept the LORD's command" (1 Sam. 13:11-14).

So Saul failed to trust God, failed to give thanks, failed to obey what he knew to be true and instead relied on his own wisdom and feelings. His not leading himself well volitionally resulted in

53

him losing everything and opening the way to years of turmoil for his family and nation, both personally and politically.

As a positive example, think of King Jehoshaphat who put a choir of praise before his inadequate army as they marched out to meet a huge invading force.

"Jehoshaphat appointed men to sing to the LORD and to praise him for the splendor of his holiness as they went out at the head of the army, saying: 'Give thanks to the LORD, for his love endures forever.'

"As they began to sing and praise, [note, they gave thanks in faith before seeing any help] *the LORD set ambushes against the men of Ammon and Moab and Mount Seir who were invading Judah, and they were defeated"* (Chron. 20:21,22).

God responded to their sacrifice of thanksgiving by fighting for them and defeating a huge enemy.

I want to add that giving thanks is not like pushing a button that makes God jump to it and help us. It means the opposite: that we are joining Him in what He's doing rather than just living in our own self-centered miniscule world. He will do what He knows is best for us, whether it be immediate relief, or having us wade through difficulties for a while yet.

Why Can We Give Thanks Before Getting an Answer?

Giving thanks in all things requires a faith based on knowledge of God's character. Reading the Word, practicing personal worship, nurturing our first love for Jesus are ways that we can expand our knowledge of the character of God. As we grow in our knowledge of how big and powerful, loving and kind, wise, just and gracious He is, we can trust Him when all looks bad. He has a plan and is working things out. *"The LORD is righteous in all his ways and loving toward all he has made"* (Ps. 145:17).

This then leads to obedience in the face of contrary evidence. To obey consistently we must have a trained will, and we train our will by making good choices in the small things of life, giving thanks in the minor irritations. He who is faithful in little will be faithful in much. Then we will be ready for the big challenges.

God Sightings

As we practice offering the sacrifice of thanksgiving, God is going to give us more of what I call "God sightings." That is, we will see Him reach into our situation and provide just what we need.

For example, we took a two weeklong trip in our 15-year-old van during a very cold spell in January with temperatures below freezing every day. In the first hour of travel, my driver's side mirror fell off and broke, leaving me blind on that side. As I responded with the sacrifice of thanksgiving, right down the road He provided a place to buy a replacement, which happened to be a convex one, giving me a much wider view of things. Later in the trip having that wider view saved me from a certain accident.

There was a second God sighting on that trip. Each day we thanked Him in faith for the protection and guidance He was going to give us and our ancient van ran well throughout the whole trip. But the day after arriving home, when I went to start it, a hose blew off the power steering unit, making the van unusable. What if that had happened on the trip, especially on some of those dark nights when we traveled narrow two lane roads with heavy traffic and no shoulder? Think of the complications and expense, the delays and difficulties that would have brought on. But when it happened in my own yard, it was just a minor problem. I had the tools and place to fix it myself, and did so quickly.

Those two God sightings showed us His protection and provision, and strengthened our faith in His goodness, power and presence. Such things happen frequently in my life, and more so as I offer the sacrifice of thanksgiving.

One wonderful side affect of having God sightings is sharing them with my unbelieving friends. I ask, "Have you ever heard of a 'God sighting?'" Even strangers are interested to hear what that is and then to listen to my examples of God sightings. This often opens the way for further conversation about spiritual things.

So, as you begin to praise in and for all things, look for an increase of God sightings in your life, and share them with others. This will strengthen your faith and deepen your love for this wonderful God who has adopted us and watches over us so graciously.

Two Lives Well Led: the Sacrifice of Thanksgiving

The buzz of conversation filled the large meeting room. The week-long conference was over and the missionaries were having last minute chats with friends they would not see again for at least a year. Soon the airport bus would come and they would all fly to their homes in various Asian countries: China, Mongolia, Japan, the Philippines and Indonesia.

While Rudy was talking to a friend, he kept an eye on his 18-month-old son, Jeremiah. Rudy and his wife, Janelle, worked in Mongolia where he taught in a university. Life there was hard with extremely cold winters, very polluted air and shortages of many things, but that was where God had called them. They were committed to living there so those who have never heard the gospel would have a chance to receive eternal life.

Rudy and Janelle had married late: he in his 50s, she in her 40s, and they were so thankful to have had a child, and a healthy one at that. Little Jeremiah was a sunny boy, happy and friendly.

Rudy watched as Jeremiah ran to one of the floor-to-ceiling windows. There was no way anyone could have known that it was unlatched. As the little boy leaned against the window to look out, it swung outward on its middle hinge and he fell forward, disappearing from sight. Rudy ran immediately to the window and looked down to see Jeremiah lying on a concrete walkway 18 feet below. He wheeled about and ran for the stairs, reaching his son in just a minute. The boy lay still. Others arrived and they scooped him up to rush him to the hospital.

The doctors there decided to operate on him immediately to relieve the swelling of his brain. However, they quickly discovered that he was more badly damaged than they thought, so they brought in his parents and other friends. As the little boy's life slipped away, Rudy broke out in the doxology, "Praise God from whom all blessings flow…." The others joined in, flooding the room with a palpable trust in the living God they all served.

The doctors stood amazed at this response of trust in God in the face of a seemingly senseless death. But for Rudy, Janelle and their coworkers, it was God at work. Within a short time after Jeremiah's last breath, Rudy and Janelle sent out an email to those who prayed regularly for them saying, "Jesus has had mercy on us and took our little boy home."

Such trust in God did not suddenly spring up in that moment. It was the result of two lives well led, soaked in the water of the Word and strengthened by many decisions to deny self in order to bring about a greater good. They were used to letting go of what they could not keep in order to receive what could not be taken from them.

Their initial godly response was like Job's after getting the news that he had lost everything he had, including all his children.

Then he fell to the ground in worship and said:
"Naked I came from my mother's womb,
and naked I will depart.
The LORD gave and the LORD has taken away;
may the name of the LORD be praised" (Job 1:20b-21)

And just as Job then had to work through his grief, so Rudy and Janelle must go through the grief cycle.[10] This cycle consists normally of 5 steps:

Denial and isolation--unable to comprehend the loss
Anger--a reaction to being helpless, vulnerable.
Bargaining--an attempt to regain control
Sadness--may lead to depression
Acceptance

But this couple had already practiced going through the cycle with small losses regularly by offering the sacrifice of thanksgiving, trusting God in the every day difficulties of life. Grasping that we have a loving Father who knows what He is doing, who has a plan and who will work it out no matter what, brings great comfort in the large losses in life.

Practice in Trust Deepens Faith

1 Peter 1:22 gives us encouragement to practice making right decisions so we become good at it: *"Now that you have purified yourselves by obeying the truth so that you have sincere love for your brothers, love one another deeply, from the heart."* Continual obedience to truth brings purification (sanctification) and a deepening love for others.

So the next time you're tempted to complain, grumble, carp or be negative, lead yourself well volitionally by participating in the power of offering the sacrifice of thanksgiving and join God in what He is doing.

As we gaze upon God in His Word, see His gracious provision and note God sightings, we get a greater grasp of His

---

[10] The Grief Cycle model first published in On Death & Dying, Elisabeth Kübler-Ross, 1969. Interpretation by Alan Chapman 2006-2013

character and can make the worldview shift needed to lead ourselves well volitionally.

A Changed View of God that can lead us to a worldview shift: Our God is all powerful, sovereign, wise and good. In His love He controls all that comes into our lives. *"Every good and perfect gift is from above, coming down from the Father of the heavenly lights, who does not change like shifting shadows"* (Jam. 1:17). What He allows is for my good, the growth of the church and for His glory. All that comes into my life is part of His great plan for the universe and He's giving me an important part to play in it, starting with offering thanks in and for all things before men and angels.

Volitional Worldview Shift: In the light of God's character, I will choose to offer the sacrifice of thanksgiving in and for all, especially for the happenings I don't like, because in doing so I can please God, cooperate with Him in removing obstacles to His work, give Him glory, and fulfill the purpose in life He's given me: to bring Him honor and enjoy Him forever.

Summary Thus Far:

Lead Yourself Well

Spiritually: add to your faith virtue by
    Nurturing your first love for Jesus.
Intellectually: add to your virtue knowledge by
    Learning to think God's thoughts, meditating on His Word.
Volitionally: add to your knowledge self-control by
    Offering the Sacrifice of Thanksgiving in every situation.

"...if you possess these qualities in increasing measure, they will keep you from being ineffective and unproductive in your knowledge of our Lord Jesus Christ" (2 Pet. 1:8)

Action Plan:
    Ask God to help you offer the sacrifice of thanksgiving, to show you the many opportunities you have every day to bring Him honor by giving thanks when you'd rather complain (your schedule is interrupted, you have a flat tire, your cell phone call is dropped, an appointment doesn't work out, your spouse is late in meeting you, the kids are cranky, the house is a mess, you have a hard

commute home, etc.) Then give thanks based on the character of God.

"Lord, I thank you for this, although I'd rather complain. I give thanks because you are good, wise, powerful and with me. You have allowed this for good in my life and I'm going to trust you by giving thanks. I praise you now for what you are going to do with this! Amen."

Chapter 9   What Does It Mean To Lead Yourself Well Emotionally?

Make every effort to...add to your self-control, endurance...." 2 Peter 1:6

"Is supper ready?" Adam called as he dropped his coat and bag in the hall and headed up the stairs. "I've got to leave by 6 for the meeting at church."

"It's almost done," answered Sue.

"AHHH!" Adam shouted. "What the heck is this? I almost tripped over this mess!"

"Oh, I was doing some extra cleaning in the bathroom and emptied everything from under the sink. Sorry," Sue replied.

"I don't know what you're thinking," Adam growled. "You should start projects like that earlier so they won't get in my way!"

"Supper's ready," Sue replied meekly. Adam came running down the stairs and slid into his place at the table.

He bowed is head and prayed, "Thank you, Lord, for this food you've provided. Amen." He looked up and snorted. "What kind of supper is this?!! I need something with some substance. You know we have this long meeting tonight. You should think more of what I need!"

Sue ducked her head, "Sorry, dear, I just wanted to try something new."

"Well, I don't appreciate being your guinea pig! Try your new things out on your friends, not me!" Adam retorted.

"Sorry, I'll do that next time."

"Good," Adam said, getting ready to take a mouthful, "Now, do you know where my book is for tonight's meeting?"

"No I don't. I haven't seen it since you brought it home on Sunday," Sue replied.

"What do you mean, you haven't seen it? You're the one who's always putting things away so I can't find them. Think about it, where did you put it?"

"What was the name of it?" asked Sue.

"*Spirituality in the Home!*" replied Adam.

Intellectually we may be followers of Christ, but, like Adam in the above scene, emotionally we are often functional atheists. That is, we say we believe in God, but act as if He didn't exist and are controlled by our emotions rather than our faith in truth. As a result, our relationships and days are often ruled by impatience, selfishness, fear, worry, anger, doubt, discouragement and jealousy. This proves hollow our claimed beliefs in God and the Bible—just ask Adam's wife about it!

Part of the reason for our being functional atheists is that emotions are both the least understood and the most influential part of our make up. We may think we operate primarily on an intellectual level, but for the most part we are kidding ourselves. Emotions are what drive us. If we better understand our emotions and God's design for them, then we can lead ourselves more effectively on the emotional level.

The Purposes of Emotions

Emotions, I believe from my observations, have three primary functions: to give pleasure, to warn us and to motivate us.

First, God gave us emotions for our enjoyment. He wants us to share in the positive feelings He has, such as joy, pleasure, happiness, delight, achievement, fulfillment, encouragement, empathy, the thrill of seeing a scene of beauty and the good feelings of healthy relationships.

We tend, however, to wander away from what God intended and fall into one of two errors. On one side, we can begin to pursue these positive emotions as an end in themselves, seeking to get more and more of them. Instead of enjoying one nice cookie, we want a dozen of them to extend the pleasure. Instead of being content with a regular day's work, we want to work extra hous for the rush of accomplishment it gives us. Instead of being content with the positive emotions of our marriage, we look for more thrills in other relationships.

We go from what is legitimate and healthy to what is selfish and destructive. This comes from getting our eyes off of Jesus and onto ourselves. What is intended to be a by-product of our walking with Him (positive emotions) becomes the focus of our lives. This is just what Satan likes, for these then become our idols.

The other error we can make is to let our negative emotions obliterate the positive ones God wants us to enjoy. In order to enjoy the beauty of emotions as God intends, we have learn to distinguish between feelings and truth. For instance, we wake up and it's raining. We had hoped for a sunny day because we are going to meet a friend for lunch and had planned to eat out on the patio of our favorite restaurant. Now we'll have to eat inside. This disappointment then becomes the emotional color of our day: grey.

However, in dwelling on this disappointment, we completely forget about all the positives the Lord is consistently pouring into our lives for us to enjoy and utilize. For instance, we slept well and when we woke up we could see, hear, stand, walk and talk. We are reasonably healthy. We are inside where it is dry. We have food for breakfast, a job to go to, money to buy lunch, a fine friend to meet with and an umbrella to keep us dry on the way. Focusing on those truths (light), rather than on our disappointment (darkness), can produce feelings of thankfulness and joy, which can then bring enjoyment of God's grace as we go through our day.

Blinking Lights

The second purpose for our emotions is to warn us. They are like the lights on the dashboard of your car. These lights, like our emotions, are not to give us guidance but to alert us that something is wrong. However, in every day life we often use our emotions for guiding us, saying things like, "I can't do that, it's outside my comfort zone!" "Today I feel like being lazy; I think I'll skip the planning meeting for Sunday School."

Think how ridiculous it would be to use a vehicle's warning lights for guidance: "Look, the oil light is on. That must mean we should turn left at the next intersection."

"Well, the check engine light is also on; I think that means we should turn right at the next road!"

Right or left doesn't matter. If you don't stop to check and correct the oil situation, you aren't going to go very far! We have to use these dashboard lights for what they're intended, as warnings, not direction.

Some of our emotions, especially the negative ones, are warning lights blinking on the dashboard of our life. Instead of letting these feelings, such as anger, disappointment, self-pity or jealousy, control us, we need to learn to use them to discern what is going on and then make the corrections needed.

For instance, if I am angry and just act out of that emotion, I'm going to do some damage to relationships. However, if I use my anger as a warning that something is wrong, I can go to the Lord, spend some time lifting my soul to him by journaling and find out what is really going on. Then I can make wise decisions of how to proceed.

How is This Lived Out?

One evening my wife made a comment that felt like a zinger—it turned out she had no intent to do "zing" me, but that's how it came across. It made me feel foolish and then angry.

I wanted to reply in kind, but instead I decided to write in my journal about how I felt. As I wrote, the Spirit pulled me up short, "See, this is the same issue we've been working on these past weeks. You are trying to get your sense of significance from your wife's words about you. That's the wrong source. You need to draw your significance from God, His love, His forgiveness, His choosing you. Don't try to get from people what only God can give! Now give thanks for this chance to step up in your spiritual growth!"

Wow, what a different perspective from my natural one! My anger was the warning sign that I was thinking wrongly. And listening to the Spirit brought understanding and prevented me from acting out of my flesh, hurting my wife and making a mess of the evening.

Here we can see again how leading ourselves well in the first areas has a big influence in the succeeding areas, like the emotional one. Spiritual leadership (nurturing my first love, focusing on Jesus), combined with intellectual leadership (memorizing/meditating on Scripture about fearing God) and volitional leadership (practicing giving thanks for what irritated me) resulted in a good decision in the emotional area to utilize the warning signal of anger (that I was trying to get my significance from what my wife thought), rather than acting out of it. The outcome was confession, repentance and joy.

In another case, I read the prayer letter of a young woman who had been my student some years earlier. She was involved in a wonderful, challenging and dangerous ministry; she described her experiences and God's answers to her prayers in vivid and well-written paragraphs. Impressive!

But what was my emotional response to this? Jealousy! Knowing that this was a totally wrong response, I immediately went to the Lord by writing in my worship journal and confessed my sins of jealousy and competition. As I wrote about this, the Spirit showed me how I was jealous of both the adventure and the acclaim this girl was having. I was not satisfied with what God had given me and was greedy for what she had. How foolish! This girl and I were both on God's team. And the fact that she was my former student meant that God had given me the privilege of building things into her life that helped her in the good work she was doing. Her success was my success!

So, with confession and repentance, my jealousy became the key to freedom from my natural and wrong perspective. You can see here again the flow from self-leadership in the spiritual realm to the intellectual, to the volitional to the emotional. As we go down the line, the force of wisdom leads us to do the right thing in the succeeding areas of self leadership.

Here are a few other examples of how an emotion can be a warning.

- ✓ Worry: I am carrying unnecessary responsibility; I am not trusting God.
- ✓ Fear: I am looking for security in the wrong place.
- ✓ Lust: I am seeking pleasure in the wrong things for the wrong motives.
- ✓ Crabbiness: I am not finding my satisfaction in Jesus.
- ✓ Complaining: I am failing to believe God, I am placing my intellect above His Word.
- ✓ Being uncomfortable: I am letting my fears, self-protection or selfishness rule.
- ✓ Lack of peace: worry, fear, discontent or failure to surrender fully to God may be controlling me. Or the Spirit may be prompting me to not do something, or to obey Him in some way.

We need to utilize our emotions, not be used by them. We need to learn to read the warning signs; more of how to do this will be explained later.

Motivation

The third purpose of our emotions is to provide motivation, encouragement and energy for us. When someone presents an idea and everyone responds with, "hmm, that's ok, but…," it usually goes nowhere. However, if one listener picks up on the idea, gives an enthusiastic response, pointing out potential positive outcomes, then others often are inspired to join in. Emotions are stirred and provide support.

Then, when we get into the midst of a project or ministry, things can get bogged down. But if one person continues to be enthused about what could come out of this, his energy and positiveness (hopefully the result of faith) can revive the commitment of the others so they can follow through to a good conclusion. This type of emotional enthusiasm is often seen in sports, hobbies and work, and God can also use it in His work, too.

Dr. Howard Hendricks, professor at Dallas Theological Seminary, told me of a man who came to talk with him after a meeting. "I'm the only Christian in my whole factory," the man said sadly, obviously feeling sorry for himself.

"Really?!!!" replied Dr. Hendricks, "You mean that God has entrusted that whole factory to you to be His light there? Why that's wonderful. What an honor!"

The man brightened up, "Really?" he asked.

"Absolutely! said Dr. Hendricks, "What a privilege He's given you."

That man went away with a very different perspective, greatly encouraged by the positive emotions Dr. Hendrick's response had stirred in him.

The other day I had a pretty severe disappointment where long promised help was, at the last minute, withdrawn. While my natural response was to grumble and slide into self-pity, the Spirit prompted me to reject these and immediately offer the sacrifice of thanksgiving. There came, then, a fierce kind of joy at this new opportunity to trust God alone when human help failed. That enthusiasm carried me through the work of processing my emotions and coming to a place of rest. And the Lord helped me move ahead with the project without that help.

Basking in Christ's Love

One way I utilize my emotions to provide encouragement and energy is in what I call "basking in the love of Christ." I do this daily while putting on the armor of God[11] (as detailed in Ephesians 6:10-18), especially in thinking about the belt of Truth, which gives us two side of the picture.

On one side is the basic truth that all I deserve naturally, in my old self, is Hell, suffering, punishment, pain and death. On the other side, God has given me exactly the opposite of what I deserve: Heaven, holiness, love, joy, peace, purpose, power, wisdom and eternal life.

As I pray through these truths, I let myself feel the wonder of going from being a condemned criminal to becoming a beloved child of God. The amazing truth is that, against all reason, He chose

---

[11] See appendix C, page 86, for an example of how to pray on the armor.

me, called me to His side, cleansed and transformed me; He claimed me as His child; He commissioned and equipped me for special service and He cherishes me. In His eyes I am dearly loved, deeply cared for, doted on and delighted in (Ps. 18:19).

These are not just cold, hard facts, they are the result of a warm, rich, heart-pounding love poured out on me from the mighty and majestic Creator of all. He wants me for His son, He is so excited about me that He sings over me! (Zeph. 3:17) And He has the same view of you.

I let that stir my emotions as I bask in the warmth of His love, exult in His wholehearted acceptance of me, rejoice in His unashamed enthusiasm for me, a redeemed sinner. This stands as a positive barrier against the natural negative thoughts I have of myself, and the condemning messages we get every day from our environment.

Here's an example from my worship journal of basking in the love of Christ.

"You, Lord Jesus, are such a beautiful God: our majestic King, our wise Shepherd, the powerful Lord, mighty Savior, gracious Brother. I love you, Lord Jesus, as you dearly love me.

"I praise you for your rich, continual, unconditional, full, whole-hearted love, which flows over me, through me, around me and goes before me every moment. There is nowhere I can go where your love does not surround me. You choose to love me, undeserving as I am; you delight in me, you sing over me, you dote on me, you deeply care for me and cherish me.

"Your love is sure, deep, powerful and strong. You love me unreservedly, enthusiastically, willfully and continually. Your love does not diminish because of my disobedience or rebellion or sin. Your love flows because of who you are, not because of what I am or do. And out of your love you will correct me when I do sin. Your love can be rested in, counted on and lived in. But it is not to be taken for granted: it is undeserved, unearned and unfathomable.

"As we see more and more of your love, Lord Jesus, we are transformed, filled with your goodness and warmed by your care. As it says in Psalm 73, 'Whom have I in heaven but you and earth has nothing I desire besides you.'

"It is so wonderful to belong to you, Lord Jesus, to be able to know you, talk with you, join you in your great plans and bask in the gracious, never-ending flow of your love. I praise you, Lord Jesus, I thank you, glorify you, rejoice in you, exalt you, my God and King, my Lord and Shepherd. May you be lifted up today in my life as I return your love in obedience to what I know pleases your heart."

Leading myself in experiencing these emotions through basking and reveling in the wonder of our God brings a transformation in my inner being. There is solidification of positive emotions, there is freedom from negative ones; there is a greater grasp of how much God loves me; and there is a greater desire to serve, obey and love Him back. This is what God desires for us. It is an ongoing process we must participate in.

Reveling Through Worship

As another positive way of stirring of my emotions, daily I turn my sights away from what He's given me onto the Lord. I do this in worship, exalting Him for who He is, and reveling in His character without thinking of how this benefits me. This focus on only Him and His greatness trains my emotions to join Truth and reject selfishness. Here's an example of one entry from my personal worship journal.

"The LORD says to my Lord: 'Sit at my right hand until I make your enemies a footstool for your feet'" (Psa. 110:1). You are wonderful, O LORD, the One glorious in holiness. You, Father, worked hand in hand with the Lord Jesus--the Sovereign One, Master, Owner of the universe, King of glory--to bring about your plan of redemption and restoration of all.

What power, what ability, what glory is at work, for you are the LORD (Yahweh whose glory is in your holiness) and the Lord (Adonai, the Owner of all who has the right to demand obedience and promises to supply all so we can obey). You will defeat evil and rebellion, eliminate lying and unbelief and bring about beauty and perfect righteousness. Your enemies will be forced to bow down before you, before Truth and Righteousness, before Justice and Mercy, before Goodness and Grace.

"The LORD will extend your mighty scepter from Zion; you will rule in the midst of your enemies" (Ps. 110:2). No enemy can defeat you, Lord Jesus, no evil can stand against you, no rebellion can succeed against you. You will prevail!

You, Lord Jesus, are the exalted One, the Most High, the Everlasting One, the Blameless One, Pure in heart, in motive, in thought, in action. All you do is good, and all you will is good. You are the Pinnacle of greatness, the Paragon of goodness, the Prince of graciousness. All must bow before such purity, such holiness, such perfection. You are worthy of praise, of trust, of obedience both now and forever more![12]

---

[12] Taken from *EDIFIED! 365 Devotionals to Stimulate Personal Worship and Spark Inner Transformation,* pp 258,259. Available at: www.edifyingservices.com and in Kindle format at www.amazon.com

Chapter 10   How Can I Lead Myself Well Emotionally?

Make every effort to…add to your self-control, endurance…." 2
Peter 1:6

"I just don't know what to do. Here are these two job possibilities and I've got to pick one soon. The sensible one is secure, plays plenty, has good benefits and I can even work from home part of the week. But it isn't really in the area I'm interested in. This other one, now, lines up with my hobby, so I'm much more attracted to it."

"What about the pay and benefits for the second job?"

"Pay is significantly less, there are no benefits and it's a long commute. But I like the work more."

"Does it pay enough to meet your budget?"

"Barely, but we could scrape by as long as there are no emergencies. It would be risky, but I'd be happier."

"Well, I'd say just follow your heart and see where the chips fall. It's better to be poor and happy than rich and unhappy."

"I agree, but my wife and six kids are urging me to take the other job."

How often do you hear the well-intended advice to "just follow your heart?" In contrast to this, God reminds us that, *"The heart is deceitful above all things, and desperately wicked; who can know it?"* (Jer. 17:9 NKJV). If we follow our heart, our emotions, we have a high possibility that we are listening to the counsel of the wicked and are heading for trouble.

In order to lead our heart well, we need to train it to follow truth. Our emotions are like a puppy. If we let our emotions run our lives, we'll get all tangled up like the puppy leash in this picture.

But if we train the puppy to heel, sit, stop and go, as well as to play in the right circumstances, it will grow into a pleasure-giving animal which can also warn us and protect us when necessary, rather than being a stress-producing tyrant that rules us. It is exactly the same with our emotions.

Critical Juncture

This is the point where we are called to add to our self-control, endurance. This is also the point where opposition comes from the world, the flesh and the devil, encouraging us to give in and give up. And it is the point at which most believers fail to stand their ground.

We know what is right and may even do it for a while, but at the same time our negative emotions push us strongly to do the wrong thing: to say a harsh word, to respond in kind rather than in grace, to indulge in lustful thoughts, to refuse to forgive or to be impatient. We need to endure through these attacks from within, standing in our commitment to truth and with our desire to please God.

When I asked a friend, who claimed to be a believer, why he wasn't going to church, he said, "I get fellowship by talking with you. I have too much to do. If I don't work Sundays I'll never get it done." In reality we were talking about 2 hours, not the whole Sunday, but it wasn't convenient for him to think about that truth.

I challenged him to go to church for a month and see how God would help him get done what was necessary. He agreed, but the first Sunday three of his friends had emergencies, all of which needed to be resolved Sunday morning! He did not recognize this as an attack of the world, the flesh and the devil and gave in to their demands. If he had put God first, rejected the emotional pressure, adding endurance to self-control, he would have been an example to his friends and have led his wife along the right path. In the end he didn't attend church once in that month.

An Example of Adding Endurance

Remember my friend, Ken, the hoarder who lived in continual chaos? One evening his son called and asked me, "What are you doing tonight?"

Knowing that a request would follow, I cautiously answered, "Well, I am working on a project. What would you like?"

"Could you take my father to Walmart? He needs to get a few things."

Since we have regular interaction with this family I knew that his father didn't "need" anything, he simply had thought of some things he wanted to get and was trying to get them now. As you remember, Ken lived a highly undisciplined life. And he did not mind making demands of others without thinking of how it impacted them. This knowledge led me to reply, "I am going to Walmart on Monday morning and I'll be glad to take your father along. Tell him so he can plan on it. Take care." And I hung up.

Immediately I began to experience negative feelings; I felt unkind, uncaring and unhappy. I liked to be the hero, to rescue people and have them think well of me. I like to please them because it makes me feel good. To say, "no" scuttled all my positive feelings. Yet I knew that if I started taking him places every time he wanted, my life would become nothing more than a taxi service. It would not be good for him or me.

My good wife helped me by telling me that I was doing the right thing even though I didn't feel like it. What she said was true, yet I felt terrible, despicable and empty. I had to continue thinking on the way of truth through the evening, offering the sacrifice of thanksgiving for this struggle and training my emotions to line up with spiritual reality. Sunday things were better as my emotions were more reasonable. On Monday I took Ken to Walmart and everything was fine.

The Cascade Continues

Our earlier commitments to lead ourselves well spiritually, intellectually and volitionally will bring strength to bear here. We can endure through our negative emotions because we know and focus on the truth, having added knowledge to our virtue and self-control to our knowledge. We can have the bigger picture that keeps us from being snared in the smaller emotional traps and details of life.

Jesus gives us the ultimate example of this. As it says in Hebrews 12:2, "Let us fix our eyes on Jesus, the author and perfecter of our faith, who, for the joy set before him, *endured the cross, scorning its shame*, and sat down at the right hand of the throne of God."

This word "endured" means to "move through with power." Jesus could do this because He did not just focus on what He felt at the moment--which was overpoweringly negative. Remember how

71

he struggled in the garden where he lifted His soul to the Father, sweating drops of blood. He said, "My soul is overwhelmed with sorrow to the point of death" (Matt 26:38). But he rejected those emotions of dread, terror and anguish, refusing to obey them and decided instead to act on truth and joy. He led His heart rather than following it.

Jesus moved through His suffering with power because He thought not just of the pain before Him, but of the joy that was to come in defeating Satan, atoning for sin and conquering death. He had the big picture in mind and focused not on the tremendous suffering of the next few hours, but on the great Plan of Redemption that He and the Father had formulated before the foundation of the world. He thought of the joy of buying forgiveness and eternal life for all.

So as we as we fix our eyes on Him, rather than our negative emotions, we, too, can move through our suffering with power, whether it be loss, betrayal, persecution, fear, sickness or death. We can have the bigger picture of knowing that God has a plan for this situation and will work it out. We can think of pleasing God, not people, of living for eternity, not the moment, of obeying truth, not our feelings. That is part of adding endurance to our knowledge.

A Secular Example

The rejection of strong but wrong feelings is illustrated on a very human level in the classic movie CASABLANCA. Set during World War II, it tells the love story of a nightclub owner and a beautiful woman who thinks her husband has been killed in the war. When the husband later turns up alive, the nightclub owner makes it possible for the woman to escape with her husband from the German police. The nightclub owner chose to be left behind, alone, in order to preserve the marriage and allow the couple to continue their resistance to the Nazi powers. What a powerful example of denying desires, leading his heart and doing what was right. He had trained his emotions to follow truth.

How Can I Lead My Heart Well?

So, what can we do to train our emotions to line up with truth rather than with what our heart tells us? The biblical concept of "lifting our soul to God" is a major means of leading ourselves well emotionally.[13]

As my soul is made up of my mind, my will and emotions, I can lift my soul to God by journaling about my thoughts, feelings and desires, letting the Holy Spirit uncover the causes of my negative emotions and what they are warning me about.

Lifting my soul to God has three aspects. First is writing out in unedited fashion what I am thinking, feeling and wanting in a particular situation. This is listening to ourselves. Second is comparing these feelings and desires with God's Word. This is talking to ourselves, speaking truth.[14] Third is surrendering to Him, committing to do what is right in the situation.[15] This is listening to God.

It is amazing what the Holy Spirit surfaces when I do this, fulfilling the truth of Psalm 143:8, "Cause me to know the way I should go, for I lift up my soul to you." Following are some examples of my lifting my soul to God, taken from my worship journal.

"Lord, I am angry and disappointed about not getting the business deal which would have brought in a good, solid income; after all those months of work, preparing the bid and doing all the research, it is a disappointment. This shows how much I've set my heart on it.

"What gripes me is that we had the low bid, which was supposed to be the deciding factor, but the state decided to let another, out-of-state bid win. That doesn't make sense! It's unjust! [This is listening to myself talk to God, being transparent in all my selfishness.]

"But, we asked you to do what is right. You are Lord, you are Master, you could easily have had it turn out otherwise [Here I am talking to myself, speaking biblical truth]. So we praise you that we did not win the bid. You have your wise reasons. Perhaps you

---

[13] This concept is presented in the Psalms: "Show me the way I should go, for to you I lift up my soul." (Ps. 143:8) and "Bring joy to your servant, for to you, O Lord, I lift up my soul. For you are forgiving and good, O Lord, abounding in love to all who call to you." (Ps. 86:4,5).

[14] This concept is from the useful book *Telling Yourself the Truth* by William Backus and Marie Chapian. Bethany House Publishers

[15] For a more complete explanation of this, see chapters 19 and 20 in my book *EQUIPPED!*

are protecting us from some harm that could have come from it.

"I thank you for what you are doing with this and I let go of it; [Here is surrender, listening to God]. I hold onto your mighty goodness and great power, knowing that you are the Wonderful Shepherd, the Provider of all we need, and God of goodness. You "are my Shepherd, I shall not want" (Ps. 23:1). So thank you that we didn't get it. I praise you again."

Did you notice what the Spirit uncovered in this lifting of my soul? I had set my heart on winning this business deal instead of on things above: "...set your hearts on things above, where Christ is seated at the right hand of God" (Col. 3:1b). I'd been caught in idol worship! The answer I got protected me from something much more serious than losing that large income.

Here's another example. "Lord, I am upset! The old used van I just bought has so many problems that it looks like it will be impossible to get it registered. I am angry—angry at myself, at the seller and at you for allowing this!

"The check engine light isn't working at all so it can't pass emissions, the gages are acting up, which probably indicates that the van's computer is going, and most importantly, the sub-frame under the front end is rotted and cracked where it's fastened to the main frame, making it dangerous to drive. Any one of those can disqualify it from being road-worthy!

"If this van can't pass inspection I will be embarrassed to have made such a bad choice, I will feel foolish. It certainly would have been a poor decision financially and otherwise—and in addition to losing the money I paid, there is all that effort on our part to travel so far to get it and the unhappiness on the part of my friend who helped me bring it home—what a waste! [I've listened to myself. Now comes talking truth to myself.]

"But, I praise you, Lord, for what you are going to do with this and for how we can trust you to work it all out. Even if I have to throw the van away, I will praise you for allowing this, for at the very least it is an opportunity to praise you by faith before all the unseen hosts.

"I confess and repent of my anger (especially the unreasonable, sinful anger towards you), of my worry, fear, lack of trust, selfishness, fear of man, pride, unbelief and rebellion. You, Lord, know what is best and will guide in all. Thank you, Lord, that you always have a sequel, that we can trust you to work out what is best even in the most hopeless of situations. I give you praise, honor and glory now for what you will do in this.

"I love you, triune God: Heavenly Father, Lord Jesus, Holy Spirit. You are pure and positive, powerful and pristine. You are good and gracious, glorious and great. You are loving and ever-lasting, lavish and lovely. To you belongs all honor, all credit, all adoration, all glory, all worship. I praise you, lift up your name, exalt you, for you, the King of Kindness, the God of Grace, the Lord of Love, you are worthy of all honor we can give you and far more—no matter what the outcome of this situation is for me. Truly, to know you, Lord Jesus, is enough for joy and I opt for that. Amen."

At the end of lifting my soul to God, I had processed my emotions, gotten a fresh vision of God and was free to proceed with life. My emotions had warned me that I was thinking wrongly, using wrong measures and being selfish. Now I could calmly and logically proceed with the possibility of registration.

In the end, the van was registered (turned out it didn't need to go through inspection, the sub-frame was still under warranty so was fixed for free, the computer was still working and a neighbor replaced the bulb for the check engine light).

The Lord worked it out—but first I had to let go of my negative emotions and move on with praise. Things don't always work out so well, but lifting my soul to God certainly brings about resolution in my emotions.

Lifting your soul, done well, also helps in the most difficult point of obedience: forgiving those who have hurt us.[16]

As we learn to lift our souls to God, processing our emotions and ending with praise, our view of God broadens and deepens so we are able to make a volitional worldview shift to walk more in truth and the freedom it brings.

A Real Story of a Young Heart Well Led

Eric sat reading his Bible, but he wasn't really concentrating. His mind kept going back to the unpleasant conversation he'd had earlier that evening with his son, Jesse. It had been a difficult one, with Jesse using "but" and "no" a great deal. There had been lots of turmoil in his demeanor along with

---

[16] For a full treatment of forgiveness, so my book *Equipped!* available at: edifyingservices.com

unhappiness and an unwillingness to admit sinful attitudes as well as incorrect thinking. He had gone to bed very early, choosing to escape any further confrontation.

"Hey, Dad,"

Eric looked up from his reading, startled. "Why hello, son, I thought you'd have been asleep long ago!"

"No," said Jesse, "I couldn't sleep so I got out my journal and spent the last two hours writing about all that we talked about. That's lifting my soul to God; I had to get it all out so I could think about it."

"That sounds like a very creative approach," said Eric, "well done!"

"As I wrote, it became so obvious that my attitude was wrong. Verses kept coming to mind, and they were all the opposite of what I was feeling. In the end I wrote eight pages with the last part being about what God thinks of my attitudes."

"Wow, eight pages!"

"There was a lot to get out." Jesse looked at the floor. "I need to ask your forgiveness, Dad, for my pride, my selfishness and my disrespect. Can you forgive me?"

Eric jumped out of his chair and hugged his son. "Of course. Thank you so much for asking, for lifting your soul to God, for listening to Him. I'm so proud of you!"

Jesse hugged his father back. "I'm so glad you gave me the book EQUIPPED! so I could learn about lifting my soul to God."

Conclusion

Lifting our souls to God is work; it takes time, determination and commitment. We probably won't do it consistently if we don't have a worldview shift. Here's some input to help yo with yours.

Changed View of God: Our God is wise, good and powerful. He made me as a whole person with mind, will and emotions. His way of integrating the three is the best, having the emotions serve my mind and will, not the other way around. He gives me power and endurance to use my emotions rather than being used by them.

Volitional Worldview Shift: As I now know the use God intends for my feelings, rather than allowing them to control me and lead me, I will use them as warnings when I should, I will enjoy those that are legitimate, and I will stimulate those which can bring enthusiasm and commitment. I will train them to cooperate with me in following Truth; I will lift my soul to God so I can discern what the warnings of my negative emotions mean.

Summary Thus Far:

Leading yourself well

Spiritually: add to your faith, virtue by
        Nurturing your first love for Jesus.
Intellectually: add to your virtue, knowledge by
        Learning to think God's thoughts, meditating on His Word.
Volitionally: add to your knowledge, self-control by
        Offering the Sacrifice of Thanksgiving in every situation.
Emotionally: add to your self-control, endurance by
        Processing your emotions through lifting your soul to God.

"...if you possess these qualities in increasing measure, they will keep you from being ineffective and unproductive in your knowledge of our Lord Jesus Christ" (2 Pet. 1:8)

Action Plan:
        Get a journal to write in. It can be a notebook, or on your computer. Then, when you have a disquieting emotion (anger, jealousy, fear, lust, pride, etc.), get out your journal and begin to write down how you feel, then process those feelings from a biblical perspective, surrendering your feelings to God and looking at them from His point of view. He will give direction.

Chapter 11   What Does It Mean To Lead Yourself Well Physically?

"Make every effort to...add to endurance, godliness...." 2 Peter 1:6

You remember my friend Ken: overweight, diabetic, disorderly, unwashed and weak. He is an outstanding example of a person who has not led himself well physically. But he illustrates only one side of the issue. On the other end of the spectrum are those who are highly disciplined and goal oriented, people who can literally work themselves to death. They may do it for money, sports or fame, but many believers also do it for ministry.

One of these was "Robert Murray McCheyne: After graduating from Edinburgh University at age fourteen in 1827 and leading a Presbyterian congregation of over a thousand at age twenty-three, he worked so hard that his health broke. Before dying at age twenty-nine he wrote, 'God gave me a message to deliver and a horse to ride. Alas, I have killed the horse and now I cannot deliver the message.'"[17]

We are called to avoid both of these extremes—being lazy or working too hard. Instead we are to care for the "horse" God gave us so we can deliver His message during all the years He has for us.

So how do I lead myself well physically? The key truth we need to grasp is that the body we live in does not actually belong to us. It is loaned to us, mostly as a means of ministry, not primarily a place of pleasure.

Just as the Israelites were commanded to care for the temple, so we are told to care for the temple of our body: *"Do you not know that your body is a temple of the Holy Spirit, who is in you, whom you have received from God? You are not your own, you were bought at a price. Therefore honor God with your body"* (1 Cor. 6:19,20). The context of this command is about avoiding sexual immorality, but honoring God with you body also includes avoiding other things that harm you physically.

As a steward of this body, I am called upon to care for and wisely utilize what God has given me in the physical realm. Because I belong to Jesus, the Holy Spirit lives in me—*"Now if anyone does not have the Spirit of Christ, he is not His,"* (Rom. 8:8b). This means my body is the dwelling place of God on earth.

Think of that: the Lord God, whose glory inhabited the

---

[17] Quoted in E. Skoglund, *Burning out for God*, p. 12, http://bible.org/illustration/killed-horse).

Tabernacle in the wilderness and the Temple in Jerusalem, now lives in us and in all followers of Jesus!

What's My Body Got to do with Godliness?

Leading myself well physically lines up with the quality of godliness in 2 Peter 1:5-7. This may seem a disconnect at first glance. However, in the cascade of growth and maturity that comes from adding to our faith virtue, then knowledge, then self-control, then endurance, the most obvious place the resulting godliness can be seen is in how we care for ourselves physically.

As our desire is to please God, we won't err on the side of harming our bodies with overeating or overworking. Nor will we be selfishly sloppy in our dress. Nor will we be overly concerned with our looks, spending lots on clothes, make-up or ego enhancing extras.

The way we care for and use our body will reflect our having led ourselves well in the other areas: in surrender to God, to His values and desires in quiet, constructive self-control. We will not follow the crowd, but the Lord Jesus. All this will show up in how we steward our body.

One Practical Application

In thinking about how I can be a good steward of this body God has given me, there are a number of practices that I should adopt. Eating well, exercising, keeping my weight at an optimum level, resting enough and taking a Sabbath each week are a few important ones. But there is one that I consider the most important single practice, one which will contribute greatly to our overall health.

The Lord brought this to my attention during the time I had to make frequent, long overseas flights. I almost always came home sick, sometimes seriously so. Then I read somewhere that the inside of an airplane in flight is one of the driest places on the planet. The air is drawn in through the engines where it is super heated and all the moisture is removed. This very dry air in the cabin then sucks the moisture out of the respiratory systems of the passengers, making them more vulnerable to the captive germs being circulated throughout the cabin.

The cure, I found, is to keep myself well hydrated, drinking lots of water before, during and after the flight. This means drinking liters of water. You have to plan for this, bringing plenty of water to drink on the way to the airport; then stocking up on water after going through security checks; and you need to also take advantage of all the water offered by the cabin crew. This will definitely result in the need to visit the bathroom a lot, but it is worth it.

Note that I said water, not coffee, tea, juice or soda, as these do not count in healthy hydration. Coffee and tea are diuretics that actually take liquid out of your body[18]; soda has lots of negatives in it, starting with a huge dose of sugar, introducing harmful things into your system, and juices also often are sugar-soaked.

Drinking some coffee and tea is fine, but if you drink too much it can lead to problems. A 30 year-old friend of mine was taken to the emergency room with serious symptoms: unable to walk, weakness, severe headache and confused in his thinking. A brain tumor? Early dementia? A stroke? No, he was simply dehydrated! He drinks lots of coffee, but not much water. Better to stick mostly with water, the real hydrator and keep your coffee and tea drinking to a couple of cups per day.

Even drinking lots of water during the flight may not in itself be sufficient—it isn't for me. So, I carry a squeeze bottle of nasal saline spray (available in any drug store), and I use it often during the flight. This makes sure my respiratory system is kept in good shape to fight off those germs. The results of doing this have been dramatic. Once I started these practices, I have rarely gotten sick on these long intercontinental flights.

This principle of hydration is important in every day life, too. Many in our country are unknowingly under-hydrated. We only drink if we feel thirsty, but most of us have trained ourselves to ignore thirst. And when we are thirsty, we drink lots of things that are harmful (as noted above in too much coffee, tea, soda or sugary juices).

It's good to drink 8 glasses of water a day. And in the winter to have a humidifier for your home, along with a hygrometer to let you know the humidity level of the air. I find that 50% is the minimum for health.

Here are some of the benefits of being well hydrated.

--As said, your nasal passages, mouth and throat will be sufficiently damp to protect you from the germs that enter.

--In drinking often you will swallow and execute a lot of germs that enter your mouth; they can't live in the acid of your stomach.

---

[18] http://bembu.com/diuretic-foods

    --Your blood will be thinner with more liquid in your body, flowing better.

    --Your hydrated blood will carry more oxygen to your whole body keeping it healthier.

    --Your brain will work better with more oxygen.

    --And your blood will more quickly carry nourishment to your cells.

    --It will also more readily carry waste away from your cells.

    -- Having more hydration in your intestines means things can move better through the digestive process, giving more nutrition and moving toxic wastes out faster.

    See this internet site for more information about this: http://themindunleashed.org/2014/09/11-reasons-dehydration-making-sick-fat.html

    This is a simple, easy way to begin caring for your body, but as we live busy lives and the forces of our culture push us towards unhealthy intake ("What would you like to drink? Soda, coffee or tea?"), it requires a commitment based on a high view of God and a worldview shift to match.

Changed View of God: God is the owner of my body. He made it so He knows what is best for it. He also redeemed it, so it is His twice over. He has now made it His temple and lives in me. He is the Creator and Sustainer of all, the Beginner and Ender of History, the King of Glory and Price of Peace. I belong to Him, my body belongs to Him and my responsibility is to care for it wisely and consistently.

Volitional Worldview Shift: Because I love God with all my heart, I will care for the body He gave me, using it first and foremost for ministry, then carefully, biblically and wisely for enjoyment and pleasure. It is the means He gave me to serve Him, and to give Him honor. Therefore I will care for it well so I can serve Him right to the end, not damage it through a selfish focus on pleasure or punishment.

Summary Thus Far

Lead yourself well

Spiritually: add to your faith virtue by
    Nurturing your first love for Jesus.
Intellectually: add to your virtue knowledge by

Learning to think God's thoughts, meditating on His Word.

Volitionally: add to your knowledge self-control by

Offering the Sacrifice of thanksgiving in every situation.

Emotionally: add to your self-control endurance by

Processing your emotions in lifting your soul to God.

Physically: add to your endurance godliness by

Caring for the body loaned you first by keeping it hydrated, then by eating wisely and exercising regularly.

"...if you possess these qualities in increasing measure, they will keep you from being ineffective and unproductive in your knowledge of our Lord Jesus Christ" (2 Pet. 1:8)

Action Plan:

Make water your primary liquid; drink several bottles a day. Cut way back on coffee and tea (one or two cups a day), limit sodas to once a week or less.

Chapter 12   What Does It Mean To Lead Yourself Well Financially?

Make every effort to…add to godliness, brotherly kindness…." 2
Peter 1:7

"Dad, I think you should get yourself a flat-screen TV. They're on sale this week. You can get a good one for only $178!

"Hmmm, I'm tempted."

"After all, Dad, you bought your present TV used 20 years ago and it was already several years old then!

"Well, son, it still works fine."

"Who knows how much longer it's going to last? Plus if you get a new one, you won't have all the complicated protocol to get your VCR and DVD player to work. The new one would have all the right plug-ins."

"If I get a flat screen, I can put it upstairs here and use it for when I do Alpha Course lessons. That would be helpful."

"So let's go and get one right now!"

"Not so fast, son. I have a policy to pray about such decisions and sleep on it before deciding. I want to make sure this is something the Lord would want me to do."

"Ok, but it sure seems the right thing to me."

--Next day--

"Well, Dad, are you going to get it?"

"No, son. I really don't need it. We can watch DVDs on my laptop if we need to. The old TV still works for any VCR tape we want to watch. And I'm not doing any Alpha Courses right now. Plus, if we have a screen up here, we'll watch it more and that isn't a good use of our time. No, we'll wait on this and use the money for the Lord's work instead."

Leading ourselves well financially involves making careful and wise decisions. Our wallet, checkbook and credit card records show what we actually value. We do what we want and buy what we value. Do our purchases line up with what we say we believe? Or do they more reflect our culture and our whims?

Well, enough of making you feel guilty. Let's go right to the most important aspect of leading ourselves well financially. We are stewards, not owners, of what we have.

We are caretakers of all that God has given us. Therefore we must think in terms of using what He has provided in ways He wants. As Paul writes in 2 Corinthians 9:11, *"You will be made rich in every way so that you can be generous on every occasion, and through us your generosity will result in thanksgiving to God."* Giving to God and others is God's main reason for giving us resources to steward.

Clarifying Questions

One way to make sure we are stewarding well what we've been given, is to ask ourselves two questions before buying anything.
"Do I need this?"
And, "Will buying this make me more effective for God?" Answering these honestly and biblically will give us guidance in stewarding what God has entrusted to us.
In the case of the flat screen TV, as I took time overnight to think on the decision, I asked the question, "Do I need this?" The clear answer was "no." Then I asked, "Will buying a new flat screen make me more effective for God?" It might if I did use it for small groups, although at present I have no small group to use it with. So after prayer and thought, both my wife and I concluded that this was not the time to buy one, even though we could easily afford it.
That's the pattern we've followed. One big reason for doing this is that we can then give more to God's Kingdom-work. That means helping fellow believers near and far as well as helping to spread the Gospel in difficult places. Since this is a high priority to God, our finances should reflect that too.

So how does brotherly kindness tie in with our finances?

If we are leading ourselves well financially, we will use our resources in a way that will help our brothers and sisters in the faith grow, deepen and mature. We will wisely help them in their physical needs. We will be supportive of them rather just nice, or tolerant or hypocritically distant.
In Ephesians 4:28, Paul emphasizes that a believer should: *"...work, doing something useful with his own hands, that he may have something to share with those in need."* And we should work

for the same reason, not just to support ourselves and our cultural desires.

We need to be aware of the needs of believers around the world and give generously through trusted organizations to help meet those needs. The less we spend on ourselves, the more we have to give away in cooperating with God in what He's doing.

When we join God in giving to the needs of others, He will tend to entrust us with more to give. As it says in Luke 6:38, *"Give, and it will be given to you. A good measure, pressed down, shaken together and running over, will be poured into your lap. For with the measure you use, it will be measured to you."*

In order to thus use God's resources wisely, wholeheartedly and consistently, we need a worldview shift.

Changed View of God: God is incredibly rich. He could manage His resources Himself, but chooses to include us in His work, giving us significant roles to partner with Him. For one of these roles He calls us to join Him in His great plan by stewarding/utilizing the resources He's bestowed on us so the needs of others can be met.

Volitional Worldview Shift: What I invest for the Kingdom of God is a double investment: it yields spiritual, social and physical dividends here in spreading the Gospel and building up the Church; plus it yields future dividends in Heaven in the rewards God will give me. Therefore I will use as much as I can of what God gives me for Him and His work.

Summary Thus Far:

Lead yourself well

Spiritually: add to your faith, virtue by
        Nurturing your first love for Jesus.
Intellectually: add to your virtue, knowledge by
        Learning to think God's thoughts, meditating on His Word.
Volitionally: add to your knowledge, self-control by
        Offering the Sacrifice of thanksgiving in every situation.
Emotionally: add to your self-control, endurance by
        Processing your emotions in lifting your soul to God.
Physically: add to your endurance, godliness by
        Caring for the body loaned you by keeping it hydrated.
Financially: add to your godliness, brotherly kindness by
        stewarding your resources for God's work.

"...if you possess these qualities in increasing measure, they will keep you from being ineffective and unproductive in your knowledge of our Lord Jesus Christ" (2 Pet. 1:8)

Action Plan:

Determine to buy less, give away more.

Ask these questions before buying: do I need this? Will it make me more effective for God?

Check your records and see if you are actually giving a minimum of 10% of your income to the Lord. If not, begin to do so.

Chapter 13   What Does It Mean To Lead Yourself Well Socially?

Make every effort to...add to brotherly kindness, love." 2 Peter 1:7

"So what does your church do for outreach?" I asked the pastor.

"Well, we are a home schooling church, so most of our people only mix with other believers. There isn't much opportunity to share their faith on a daily basis."

Hmmm, doesn't seem to match up with the way Jesus dealt with life. As I understand it, there are two basic reasons that God leaves us here on earth after we become His children. First is worship leading to maturity. He gives us the opportunity to praise and glorify Him as we move through trials and tribulations designed to conform us to the image of His Son. As it says in James 1:2-4 *"Consider it pure joy, my brothers, whenever you face trials of many kinds, because you know that the testing of your faith develops perseverance. Perseverance must finish its work so that you may be mature and complete, not lacking anything."* (Emphasis mine)

Second, flowing from the first, we are left here to be a witness of His goodness to all those who don't yet know Him, giving them opportunity to become believers, too. Jesus emphasized this in his last teaching on earth, giving us the command to *"...go and make disciples of all nations..."* (Matt. 28:19a).

We cannot accomplish this second responsibility if we have no social relationships with unbelievers. Jesus is our example in this: He spent time with people in every level of society, in every category of morality, in every part of the religious spectrum. Like Him, we need to intentionally mix with people who don't yet know Jesus, as well as with our fellow believers.

I want to focus here on what I consider the primary aspect of leading yourself well socially, one which will determine how well we will be able to fulfill Jesus' desire for us to both worship Him and to be an effective witness for Him.

What is This Most Important Aspect?

The most foundational thing we can do in leading ourselves well socially is to discern where we are controlled by the fear of man and replace it with a fear of God.

Proverbs 29:25 says, *"Fear of man will prove to be a snare, but whoever trusts in the LORD is kept safe."* Fear of man is basically giving too much importance to the opinions of those around us. It is letting others decide for us what we should value, what we should and shouldn't do, how we should dress and what we should say.

We all operate under this influence to some degree. Who wants to wear clothes that are totally out dated and weird? Vintage polyester from the 70s, anyone?

There is some measure of conformity in outward forms that is healthy—if we were so out of touch with reasonable norms for dress and speech that everyone saw us as total eccentrics with nothing to say to them, we'd be useless in our witness. However, our inner, core values, actions and speech should not come from those around us but from our awe of and love for God. If our core values are the reason people reject us, then that is OK. In fact, this is what Jesus predicted: if they rejected Him, they will reject us.

To fear God does not mean to grovel before Him in terror all the time. It means basically that we are in awe of His greatness and that we respect Him deeply; it means that we do not want to hurt Him and therefore obey Him. It also means we are afraid of the just consequences of disobeying Him. Basically to fear Him is to obey Him--from the right motives.

In fearing Him, we highly respect Him: His wisdom, goodness, knowledge and power. Out of our love for Him we want to do what He desires. We love Him because He first loved us and we have a strong interest in bringing Him honor.

If we truly fear Him, we will care what He thinks about what we do, say, think and spend time on. Such a strong commitment to what the Ruler of the universe thinks can set us free from the tyranny of others' opinions.

We are all familiar with verses emphasizing the great benefits of the fear of the Lord.[19] One powerful presentation of this

---

[19] "The fear of the LORD is pure, enduring forever" Psa. 19:9.

"The fear of the LORD is the beginning of wisdom; all who follow his precepts have good understanding" Psa. 111:10.

"The fear of the LORD is the beginning of wisdom, and knowledge of the Holy One is understanding" Pro. 9:10.

"The fear of the LORD adds length to life, but the years of the wicked are cut short" Pro. 10:27

"The fear of the LORD is a fountain of life, turning a man from the snares of death." Pro. 14:27

"The fear of the LORD leads to life; Then one rests content, untouched by trouble" Pro. 19:23

is found in Psalm 34:8-10. It begins with, *"Taste and see that the LORD is good; blessed is the man who takes refuge in him. Fear the LORD, you his saints, for those who fear him lack nothing. The lions may grow weak and hungry, but those who seek the LORD lack no good thing."* The basic message here is that fearing God is the doorway to His provision flowing into our lives!

Then in verse 11 comes an enticing invitation and hint of a promise: *"Come, my children, listen to me; I will teach you the fear of the LORD. Whoever of you loves life and desires to see many good days..."* will fear God (Psa. 34:8-11). If we fear the Lord, it will profoundly affect our lives for good, giving us many days in which we will see good. This is what the Lord wants for us, offers us and calls us to. Our part is to see Him in His greatness and stand in awe of Him, not people.

Verse 13 gives the exact description of what it means to fear God: *"keep your tongue from evil, your lips from speaking lies. Turn from evil and do good, seek peace and pursue it."* Let's look briefly at each one of these statements.

"...keep your tongue from evil...." To fear God means we want to be like Him and speak what is good and edifying. Gossip, negative talk, destructive statements are all off limits for us. We are to be in the process of joining God in building up, encouraging and comforting people, not tearing them down.

"...and your lips from speaking lies." God is truth; we want to speak what is of Him. By knowing God's Word well, we can discern the lies that our culture, our friends, our church, and we tell ourselves. Then we can replace these lies with Truth.

"Turn from evil and do good;" In fearing God, we give no place for evil in our lives, we seek to do what God would do, which is only good. This has to do with our daily life, dress, values, activities, how we spend our time and money as well as what we watch and read.

"...seek peace and pursue it." As we fear God, we will deal with conflicts rather than letting them fester. We will seek to bring peace in every relationship; if we fail, it should be because the other person refuses to move ahead, not because we are stubborn and

---

"Humility and the fear of the LORD bring wealth and honor and life" Pro. 22:4.

"He will be the sure foundation for your times, a rich store of salvation and wisdom and knowledge; the fear of the LORD is the key to this treasure" Isa. 33:6.

unforgiving, or overly demanding.

How Does This Relate To Love?

If we fear God and not people, our interactions with our fellow believers will take on a new depth characterized by God's love flowing through us to them. We will value relationships above things. We will be free from following people and be leaders instead. We will be transparent, real, vulnerable followers of Jesus, reaching out to help others along the way.

We are offered the opportunity to show God's love to the unreached peoples of the world by sharing the gospel through our lives. If we walk in the fear of man, we will be hesitant to speak of Jesus, to share our faith, to even mention spiritual things, as these are "off limits" in western society.

However, if we fear God, are concerned with what He thinks and live in the unseen truth that those around us need Christ, we are going to speak up whether it's acceptable or not. We are thinking, with God, about the eternal consequences of not knowing Christ. Therefore we will do whatever we can to make sure those around us know about Jesus and what He has done to provide salvation and eternal life for all.

The more we know of God's greatness and glory, the more we will stand in awe of Him. And the more our awe grows (and it should), the less we will be affected by the opinions, fears and hang-ups of those around us. Like Jesus, we will want to relate to all who come our way, to show love, grace and goodness so that these people may come to know Christ.

In Conclusion

In this last area of leading ourselves well socially, our focus is on God, His great love, His gracious goodness, His abundant provision, His high and holy character. This is a relational thing, not a legalistic thing. Our doing flows out of His reaching out to us and results in our loving Him back.

As in every other area of self-leadership, we will only make a change in whom we fear if we have a shift in our worldview based on a new understanding of God. Here's what we need.

Changed View of God: El Elyon, the most High God is awesome: His power is beyond comprehension; His knowledge is beyond measure; His wisdom in without limit; His authority is absolute. He is the most important One in the whole universe, totally above any other: all others are created but He is the Creator. He is the One who made me, called me to be His child and has commissioned me to the high calling of being His ambassador to all around me.

Volitional Worldview Shift: The most High God is the One whose approval I will crave, whose opinion matters and whose values I want to live by. I choose to give Him supremacy in my life, shown in obedience and honor, rather than being a slave to what the people around me think or value or do. I choose to fear the Living and True God.

Summary Thus Far

Lead yourself well

Spiritually: add to your faith, virtue by
   Nurturing your first love for Jesus.
Intellectually: add to your virtue, knowledge by
   Learning to think God's thoughts, meditating on His Word.
Volitionally: add to your knowledge, self-control by
   Offering the Sacrifice of thanksgiving in every situation.
Emotionally: add to your self-control, endurance by
   Processing your emotions in lifting your soul to God.
Physically: add to your endurance, godliness by
   Caring for the body loaned you by keeping it hydrated.
Financially: add to your godliness, brotherly kindness by
   stewarding your resources for God's work.
Socially: add to your brotherly kindness, love by
   Rejecting the fear of man, acting from the fear of God.

"...if you possess these qualities in increasing measure, they will keep you from being ineffective and unproductive in your knowledge of our Lord Jesus Christ" (2 Pet. 1:8)

Action Plan:
   Memorize Proverbs 29:25, *"Fear of man will prove to be a snare, but whoever trusts in the LORD is kept safe."* Then when you sense negative pressure to conform to the world, think about what God would have you to do in that moment; volitionally reject the fear of man and care what the Creator of the universe thinks.

Chapter 14 So, What's Next?

In order to bring change we need God's help, and we get His help through prayer. In this short chapter I want to share two prayers which can assist you in the application of the things you've learned thus far. Such prayers are what I call "Truth Transporting Liturgies."

As we pray them often, the truths within are deeply planted in our souls. You can also pray such prayers for others and be sure the Lord will answer them powerfully, for you are praying His will.

Praying with Peter

The first one is praying through 2 Peter 1:5-7, asking God to make this passage true in your life. I find that memorizing such a passage and praying it from memory has me interacting with it on a deeper level than just reading it.

Here's what I would pray. "Lord, I praise you for all that you have provided for me to live a godly life. Help me to be eagerly diligent to add to your gift of faith, *virtue*. I surrender myself afresh to you, agreeing to obey what you've taught me and what you will teach me. May I nurture my first love for you, seeing more of you each day.

"Help me to add to my virtue, *knowledge*, being diligent to read, study and meditate on your Word so I can think your thoughts. May your Holy Spirit open my eyes to what I need to learn.

"Help me then to add to my knowledge, *self-control.* Help me to eagerly obey what I know to be true, starting with thanking and praising you in all things.

"Then as obstacles, problems and hardships come, help me to add to my self-control, *endurance.* As I move through my problems with power, trusting you to work things out, help me to lift my soul to you, processing my emotions so I can use them as you intended. Protect me from being controlled by my emotions. Help me instead to utilize and lead them.

"As I look to you for assistance, help me then to add to my endurance, *godliness*, becoming like you. May this be seen in the way I care for this body you have given me, for it is your temple.

"Then help me to add *brotherly kindness* to my godliness, seeing my brothers and sisters as you do with eyes of compassion and wisdom. Guide me in using the resources you have given me to steward to help others.

"And finally help me to add to my brotherly kindness agape *love*, loving others as you do. Help me to reject the fear of man and instead walk in awe of you, obeying you with all my heart, speaking wisely and boldly as you direct.

"I praise you now for how you will answer me in this. Amen"

Praying with Paul

Another powerful passage is the prayer of the Apostle Paul for the Colossians, found in the first chapter of his book to them. This prayer contains most of the seven elements of leading yourself well. Paul writes:

"For this reason, since the day we heard about you, we have not stopped praying for you and asking God to fill you with the knowledge of his will through all spiritual wisdom and understanding.
"And we pray this in order that you may live a life worthy of the Lord and may please him in every way: bearing fruit in every good work, growing in the knowledge of God,
being strengthened with all power according to his glorious might so that you may have great endurance and patience, and joyfully
giving thanks to the Father, who has qualified you to share in the inheritance of the saints in the kingdom of light.
"For he has rescued us from the dominion of darkness and brought us into the kingdom of the Son he loves,
in whom we have redemption, the forgiveness of sins."

Here's an example of how I would pray this, arranging the truths in line with the seven areas of self-leadership.
[Spiritual] "Lord Jesus, as I get to know you more and more through your Word, seeing the beauty and bounty of your being, I want to live a life worthy of you and to please you in every way. Help me to do that. As I surrender myself to you, guide and direct me.
[Intellectual] In order to please you, I ask that you fill me with the knowledge of your will through all spiritual wisdom and understanding. Help me to grow in my knowledge of you; speak to me as I am in your Word every day.
[Volitional] Help me to be constantly and joyfully giving thanks to you, Heavenly Father, especially for your qualifying me to be a

partaker of the inheritance of the saints in the Kingdom of light.
[Emotional], Strengthen me each day with all power according to
you glorious might that I might have great endurance and
patience,
[Physical, financial and social] Help me to be bearing fruit in every
good work, remembering that you have rescued me from the
dominion of darkness and have brought me into the Kingdom of
your son whom you love, in whom I have redemption, the
forgiveness of sins. May I be ever sharing this gracious truth
with those around me. Amen.

You will find other passages to pray as your read consistently
through the New Testament.

Chapter 15   How can I expand my obedience?

With the basics in place, we have a framework to add other aspects of leading ourselves well. Following here are several things we can cultivate in each of the seven areas. At the top of each list I will repeat the most important element.

I will give brief explanations of the points which contain concepts that may be new to you. For deeper understanding of these concepts, I would refer you to my book *EQUIPPED!* available in paperback at www.edifyingservices.com, and as a kindle edition on Amazon under the title *Knowing Jesus Is Enough For Joy, Period!* These points will have two stars (**) before them.

I would encourage you to include whatever points you find useful and relevant at this time of your life. Then look for further points to add as the Lord matures you and opens your eyes through Scripture, prayer, advice and experience. And always be looking for opportunities for volitional worldview shifts.

Keep clearly in mind that all must be measured by Scripture, not by culture, our heart or our church. Only as we live in Scripture can we stay on the path laid out in 2 Peter 1.

Leading myself well Spiritually: Adding virtue (surrender) to my faith
- Nurturing my first love for Jesus
- **Being filled with the Spirit daily (confessing any known sin and asking for the filling of the Spirit, surrendering to His leadership).
- **Dealing with the next sin: paying attention to what the Holy Spirit is convicting/pointing out in my life, immediately repenting and abandoning it.
- **Confessing in layers: seeing that sins like worry or impatience are only the top layer of a series of sins that all need to be confessed in order to deal with the top one effectively. For example, under worry are: fear, failure to surrender, refusal to trust God, pride, selfishness, unbelief and rebellion. We need to confess down through those to be free of worry.
- **Discerning and purifying motives: doing the right thing for the wrong motive can spoil it. We always have mixed motives and need to spot and reject the wrong and neutral ones, acting only on the positive ones. This can be done as part of lifting your soul to God through journaling.

- **Asking for and cultivating ongoing revival—seeing more of God's greatness, then of our depravity and through this growth in understanding, getting a greater grasp on the wonder of God's forgiveness and love for us.
- **Forgiving and asking forgiveness—the highest forms of obedience.

Leading myself well intellectually: Adding knowledge to virtue
- Memorize and meditate on God's word; think His thoughts. (See Appendix A for further explanation).
- Have biblical expectations: distinguish between cultural ones (that all should go well with me, that I deserve only good) and biblical expectations (I'm in a spiritual war, Satan will attack, I will be opposed and persecuted when I stand for Christ. Along with the pleasant things God has for me I will experience suffering and difficulties which come to mature and deepen me,).
- Read widely—avoiding what pollutes
  Christian books
  Secular books
  News—use this for prayer fuel.

Leading myself well volitionally: Adding self-control to knowledge

- Praise God in and for all things.
- Be alert to potential volitional worldview shifts—listen to the gentle reprimands of the Spirit and the Word as well as godly advisors.
- **Let go, Hold on, Rise above. Learn to let go of what is temporal, hold on to what is eternal, and you will be able to rise above what is petty, selfish and negative, above the thoughts and attacks of others, above problems, difficulties and distress. Based on Colossians 3:1,2.
- Realize that small decisions count. Discipline in the small things (flossing your teeth, keeping things orderly, being on time) prepares you for making big decisions well when crises come.
- Measure how long it takes to do what you are reluctant to do (flossing your teeth, washing dishes, cutting your nails); often it takes much less time than it seems and you can use that to motivate you to do what you should.
- Spot and reject laziness.

- Pamper yourself by doing what is right rather than what is unhealthy or negative!

Leading myself well emotionally: Adding endurance to self-control
- **Journal, lifting your soul to God: processing your emotions in the light of Scripture.
- Intentionally practice using your emotions for pleasure, for warning and for motivation.
- **Learn to quickly recognize warning signs of when emotions are leading you rather than you leading them; know your weaknesses and guard against them: my prime one is self pity.
- Reject the urge to be a victim or victor; instead be a vector, pointing others to God. A victim's life is defined by his suffering; his defining emotion is self-pity: he must blame someone else rather than taking responsibility himself. Joseph in the cistern was a victim. A victor's life is defined by his success; his defining emotion is pride: the result is his fall. In Potiphar's house Joseph was a victor and he ended up in prison. A vector's life is defined by his relationship to God; his defining emotion is thankfulness: he is a signpost, pointing people to God. When Joseph stood before Pharaoh, he was a vector, saying "I cannot interpret your dream….but God will give Pharaoh the answer he desires" (Gen 41:16).

Leading myself well physically: Adding to my endurance, godliness-- evidencing the values of God in the way you care for His temple, your body.
- Drink more water
- Minimize intake of coffee, tea, soda, sugary juices
- Take care of your body so you can use it for God, keeping your weight at an optimal level, keeping it strong and healthy by doing the following.
- Eat well:
    - eat enough(lots of) fiber. Avoid the pain of diverticulitis;
    - Eat less: learn your triggers that lead to excess eating; use smaller plates, eat slowly;
    - avoid white sugar, white flour, salt;
    - keep sweet deserts to a minimum, one small helping; prefer something healthy, like fruit.
    - eat healthy snacks: fruit, veggies, popcorn

- Exercise
  - Walk more
  - Climb stairs
  - Have an exercise program if that helps you.
- Sleep enough
  - Aim for 8 hours of sleep
  - Earlier to bed, earlier up
  - Avoid what inhibits sleep (sitting in front of screens right up until you go to bed, etc).

Leading yourself well financially: Adding brotherly kindness to godliness

- View yourself as a steward of all God gives
- Simplify
- Buy less, buy used
- Be aware of and reject greed, and selfishness.
- Reject get rich quick ideas.
- Give away more; see needs, meet them wisely.
- Ask God for more to give away.
-

Leading myself well socially: Adding agape love to brotherly kindness
- Always be on the lookout for and reject the fear of man in your life. It's there, often disguised as something else (caution, wisdom, being nice, not making waves, etc.).
- Ask for and look for chances to share about your warm and wonderful walk with Jesus. Be an example in life; also speak up.
- Share Jesus Sightings with everyone.
- Make friends with sinners!
- Have friends in all levels of society.
- Start Bible studies for nonbelievers, and for believers.

Appendix A   Meditation[20]

In my early twenties I was able to attend a Bill Gothard seminar[21] and found it very helpful. The first time I went, Bill's teaching impacted me in two ways. First was how he took Scripture as truth, accepting what it had to say at face value. That may seem like a statement of the obvious to believers, but I found that I was picking and choosing what to really believe—that is, to implement in my life. I was convicted specifically that when it came to forgiving and asking forgiveness, I wasn't applying God's directions one bit. When I obeyed Scripture in this area there was release and a new freedom.

The second powerful application was meditation. Bill's presentation of this and the illustrations from his own life impressed me greatly, and I determined to apply it in my own life. Bill gave us a list of ten chapters to begin with and offered us a free book if we completed these. That incentive, however, had no motivating effect on me compared with the desire to cooperate with God in learning His Word.

Meditation is essentially cooperating with God in the transformation of our souls. As we have mentioned, the three major parts of our souls are our mind, our will, and our emotions. Meditation is working with the Holy Spirit to bring change in each of these areas.

Psalm 1 gives some insights into meditation. Interestingly, it begins by telling us three sins to avoid, which correspond basically to the first three parts of the armor of Ephesians 6:10-18. Psalm 1 begins, "Blessed is the man who does not walk in the counsel of the wicked. . . ." Those reject ungodly advice, taking instead the counsel of God who are blessed; their relationship with God is protected by keeping on the *belt of truth.*

". . . or stand in the way of sinners . . ." Knowing that the way of sinners would lead to great inner conflict with themselves, they reject it, thus keeping on the *breastplate of righteousness.*

". . . or sit in the seat of mockers." Instead of mocking and attacking verbally those the godly don't like or agree with, they forgive them, thereby putting on the *shoes of peace.*

---

[20] Quoted from my book, *Equipped: Ready for Everyday Spiritual Warfare,* (Edifying Press, 2013) pp. 269-275

[21] For information on Bill Gothard's Institute in Basic Life Principles, see www.iblp.org and check out especially the Embassy Institute where you can easily see the teachings I was able to attend.

Then the second verse gives us two positive things the godly person does: "But his delight is in the law of the LORD, . . ." God's Word is what this person revels in, rejoices in, delights in. This means that when his or her mind is free, what comes to it is God's Word. It is a great source of joy. We can tell when we delight in something or someone by noticing how we spontaneously think and talk about them. Think sports, think work, think about when you first met your spouse.

". . . and on his law he meditates day and night." Second, godly people meditate on God's Word regularly, frequently, continually. It means that they have memorized it so they can think on it at any time, and they refer to it often.

The outcome of avoiding the three sins and implementing the two positives is laid out in verse 3: "He is like a tree planted by streams of water. . . ." The roots of this person have grown deep down into the water of God's Word, drawing refreshment, sustenance, strength, and vitality from it all the time.

". . . which yields its fruit in season. . . ." The result of the continual watering is that whatever fruit the godly person needs to bear will come forth. Consider the fruit of the Spirit: if the situation calls for patience, it will be there; if faith is needed, that will be there.

". . . and whose leaf does not wither." No matter what the circumstances around him or her may be, the godly person will remain fresh and vital. I have seen in the Middle East two trees not far apart. One twisted and dried without a single leaf, for it grew fifty yards from the stream; when a drought came, it died. The other tree grew next to the small stream, getting its roots down into the wet soil, deep into the earth. When all else was brown, its leaves were still a rich green, making it stand out from its surroundings.

"Whatever he does prospers." This is the astounding outcome: *whatever* godly persons do will prosper. Not just some things, but whatever they do. This is true, not because they are wise or talented or diligent. It is true because in meditation they have learned to think like God and to trust Him fully and thereby to obey His direction. They have internalized the truths needed for life.

I have witnessed such fruitfulness in the lives of those I know who practice meditation. It is not that meditation is magic, but that meditation is cooperation with God in bringing transformation that allows Him to cmpower, guide, and protect in a greater way than for those who fail to take the time to meditate. The meditator is then going to make decisions in line with God's will, using the wisdom of God's Word to avoid things that will prevent prospering.

The "How to" of Meditation

Meditation has three parts. The first is to memorize the passage. This is cooperating with the Holy Spirit in the *transformation of our minds.* It is learning to think God's thoughts. This is the mechanical part, but it is necessary to begin the internalization of truth.

Second is to personalize it, putting personal pronouns in where you can. This is cooperating with the Holy Spirit in the *transformation of our emotions.* Personalizing Psalm 1:1 would be to say, "Blessed am I when I don't walk in the counsel of the wicked, when I don't stand in the way of sinners, when I don't sit in the seat of the scornful."

When I read Scripture, it is like looking at a powerful river flowing by. When I personalize the passage, it is like that river flows over me, bringing its power and cleansing into my life.

The third part is to pray through it. This is cooperating with the Holy Spirit in the *transformation of our will.* Praying Psalm 1:1 would be to say, "Blessed am I when I don't walk in the counsel of the wicked. Lord, help me to recognize the counsel of the wicked and then to reject it. Help me to recognize your counsel and to implement it." This is a surrender to God's will, giving Him your will and taking His in its place. Since you are praying for exactly what God wants — praying Scripture, after all, is asking for the clear will of God — He is going to answer that prayer.

Such meditation brings powerful, deep, foundational change in us. I can honestly say that meditation has been the most important source of spiritual, intellectual, and emotional growth in my life. If I hadn't known how to meditate, I never would have made it for thirty years in the Middle East; I would have been chewed up and spit out by the forces of evil. Meditation has resulted in exactly the opposite happening: all that the Lord has put my hand to has prospered—not immediately, but in the long run. This is the Lord being faithful to His Word, not my being successful in my talents and strengths. All glory must go to Him for fulfilling His promises and purposes.

Illustrations

In an analogy illustrating meditation, think of a piece of tough beef. We can eat it as is, but it is difficult to chew and get it down. This is like reading the Word; there are some difficult things in the Bible and much that we don't know how to implement.

Second, if we dip the meat into a bowl of marinating sauce for five minutes, it will change the taste but not the texture of the meat. This is like study. We still have a lot of questions about how to implement it; we have an intellectual grasp but not necessarily a heart change.

However, if we put the meat into the sauce and leave it there for forty-eight hours, the sauce penetrates to the center of the meat, transforming both its texture and its taste. This is like meditation, which results in transformation of our soul, our relationship with God, our family life, and our work for Him.

Or, to use a second analogy, think about going to the beach. You spread out your towel on the sand, lie on your stomach, and watch the waves. The sunlight sparkles on the water; the waves roll in unceasingly, each one a bit different; some sea gulls fly overhead, puffy white clouds dot the sky — it is an inspiring scene. This is like reading God's Word: uplifting, refreshing, edifying.

Then it gets hot, so you jump up and run into the water, enjoying the coolness. You ride the waves in, and swim out for another try. This is like studying the Word: you are really "into it." It is decidedly different than lying on the beach and watching the water.

After a while you decide to put on your mask and snorkel and go underwater. As you dip below the surface and swim over a ridge, whole new worlds open up to you that could not be seen from the beach or while swimming in the waves: schools of fish, various types of seaweed, brightly colored creatures clinging to the rocks. This is like meditation; it gets you down below the surface into the depths of the Word. It reveals to us things we would probably never see in reading or study. And it provides the application of these truths in our lives through prayer.

Let me give you a simple example of how meditation helps us to see into the depths of Scripture. I memorized Psalm 23 when I was about five years old, and I have used it many times to encourage myself. Once while meditating on it (praying through it while personalizing it), a new point jumped out at me from verse 6: "Surely goodness and mercy shall follow me all the days of my life" (KJV). God promises goodness and mercy, but they *follow* us, so we often cannot see them when walking through difficulties. Later, however, as we look back, we can see how God was pouring mercy on us and working things out for good.

That was a really helpful insight, leading me to greater faith in God when in difficulty and giving more ability to praise when there is no visible reason to praise. I doubt that I ever would have noticed this detail in merely reading or studying.

Helpful hints

Here are several practical ideas for implementing meditation in your life.

• Have a partner to encourage you. It's easy to begin well, but it's also easy to have your resolve peter out. Memorizing is hard work, and we naturally shy away from it. To make ourselves accountable to someone can help keep us on track, especially if you and your partner are both memorizing the same passage.

• Memorize passages (paragraphs or whole chapters), not just verses. This gives you the context and the flow of what God is saying.

• Memorize a verse or two a day until you have the passage down well. Taking bit-sized chunks makes this a doable task. Doing it at the same time each day also helps—for example, making memorization part of your quiet time, then reviewing what you've memorized in the evening. Also, try to visualize a picture to go with the verse. That's easy with Psalm 1, as it is stated as a series of word pictures.

• After you have the passage memorized, meditate through it (personalizing and praying it) each day for two, three, or four weeks, letting it soak down into your soul.

• Avoid mechanical repetition; connect with the Word, think about it as you meditate, and pray creatively.

• Periodically review passages you have meditated on earlier, not because you should, but because you love God and His Word (that is, you have good motives). I "cycle through" the chapters I've memorized every once in a while to keep them fresh.

• When you experience any difficulty in life, go to a passage that speaks to it and memorize and meditate on it. For instance, I find that in the conflicts I have had with people, Psalm 37:1-10 has been a wonderful refuge, a boost, and a road map of how to respond. Meditating on it always gives me what I need to move ahead.

• When you have a difficulty, it is much easier to memorize a new passage that speaks to your situation than to memorize one that is theoretical at that point in your life.

Here are some passages to start with:

- Psalm 1: God's way to success
- Psalm 23: the all-purpose passage
- Psalm 37: how to respond to conflicts
- Psalm 46: dealing with difficulty
- Psalm 62: God's perspective on life
- Psalm 73: dealing with envy
- Psalm 86: the balance between weakness and God's power
- Matthew 5–7: thinking God's thoughts
- Ephesians 1: the eternal perspective
- Colossians 3: thinking God's values
- Hebrews 12:1-17: difficulties—why they come, what to do with them
- 1 Peter 1 and 4: purposes for suffering

Once you have memorized some of these, you will see other passages in Scripture that you would like to meditate on. As you memorize, give them a title, as that will help you in the process. Once you have memorized and meditated on a passage, you will have a "gift" to give to others who are struggling with something. You can turn to a relevant passage and share from the treasures you have gleaned in your meditation.

So, commit yourself to an adventure with Jesus in mediating on Scripture and see where He takes you!

Appendix B   Examples of Personal Worship

I praise you, Lord, that when I awoke this morning, you were there, watching, protecting, waiting. I praise you that in you is all we need, for you have created us to "dock" with you. Without you we are unplugged, adrift, lost and harmful to the environment. With you we are in place, empowered, employed and enjoyed.

You, Lord God, are the Master Planner, the Mighty Architect, the Magnificent Creator and the Majestic Concluder of all. You are wonderful, wise, willful and One. In you there is harmony, wholeness, holiness and happiness. With you there is potential, power, protection and provision. In you we can trust, tremble, and triumph. In you, with you and from you comes all that we will ever need.

You are majestic, marvelous, beautiful and greatly to be praised. I exalt your Name, I magnify your Character, I rejoice in your Goodness and honor your Greatness. You are worthy of all worship: whole-hearted, unified, total-commitment praise, honor and obedience.

May this be true in my life today, Triune Lord God, Ruling Heavenly Father, Commanding King Jesus, Guiding Holy Spirit. May you be lifted up before all around me, may you be exalted in my motives, attitudes, words, actions and interactions today. Amen.

****

Praise be to you, Lord, for a new day, a clear sky, the promise of warmth and beauty. I praise you, Lord God, my Heavenly Father, Jesus my Shepherd , my indwelling Holy Spirit, that all beauty flows from you, that all of today is in your hand. We can trust you a thousand percent, for in your character, in your core, in all your being there is only goodness, wisdom, purity, perfection and positive power. You have no evil, no darkness, no dark side, no selfishness, no sin, no negatives, no unrighteousness.

You are the absolutely trustable One, ever watching to protect, guide, correct and keep your beloved children on the right track. I thank you, Lord, for your constant presence, your consistent protection, your unending attention, your unlimited power.

You are the One to be loved, to be obeyed, to be exalted, to be praised. You are worthy of continual worship, adoration and obedience. May these things be present in my life today so that your name may be lifted up before men and angels, before demons and the devil. Amen.

****

I praise you this morning, Lord, for your steadiness in the face of my floundering. I am up and down, both diligent and lazy, productive and useless, strong and weak, spiritual and selfish, kind and harsh, disciplined and rebellious.

I give you praise that you are so unlike me, that every day you are the same in your character, your heart, your plans, your love. Each morning when I awake, my emotions are jumbled, my thoughts are full, my impressions from yesterday are varied, but you are the steadily the same, ever the same: gracious, great, glorious and unyieldingly, unwavering, unbelievably good.

Being thankful for this is not enough: you are Someone to be ecstatic about, the One to be celebrated, rejoiced in, exalted and worshiped. To turn our inner eyes away from self, the world and all that is in it to You is to go from darkness to light, from weakness to strength, from groveling on the streets of life, to walking with the King of creation. You are such a contrast from the weak and temporary things we have here. You are the Creator and Sustainer of all, the Preparer of a new heaven and earth, the Ender of history and the Essence of eternity.

In you is endless beauty, unfathomable love, unsearchable wisdom, inscrutable holiness and unending goodness. In you we can rest in security, in you we can live in light, in you we can know Truth, in you we can be abundantly accepted, lavishly loved, completely cherished and deeply delighted in.

I can praise you now for what will come today, Lord Jesus, for you have prepared it all, will guide in all, will provide in all. I can rest in the richness of your character, be at peace in the provision of your grace, bask in the light of your love and rejoice in the certainty of your presence. You have given me all joy and peace in yourself. What more could I need? Nothing! You are far more than sufficient and I rest in, rejoice in, respond in the wonder of being your undeserving but beloved child.

****

Praise you, Lord, for your gracious and kind hand at work in my life. I give you glory for your rock solid goodness, your whole-hearted holiness, your deep, continual steadiness. You do not vacillate the way I do, you do not sin and suffer remorse, you do not stray off the path of righteousness and need correction as I do.

I praise you for your immutability, your perfection, your flawlessness. In you there is surety, in you there is certainty, in you there is eternal, unshifting, beautiful purity. You are the One, the only One, upon whom I can lean, for you will never change and will never let me down.

You are the great and gracious One, ever active in my life, correcting, directing, protecting, empowering. When I stray, you are there to prick, convict and correct, bringing me back to the Path of peace and the Rock of rest.

It is so comforting, so encouraging, so gracing to live in your powerful presence, your lavish love, your awesome acceptance and your righteous rule. I look out over the sketch of today, just a few bare points of possibility visible to me, but at the same time you, Lord, see every detail of what will happen in full color, every dimension, total outcome. Therefore I can rest in the fact that for you there are no surprises, you can guide me through every twist and turn, every problem and possibility. You prepare me, bringing to mind what should be done, what I should remember and what I should avoid. Praise you, Lord, for your complete love, your competent preparation, your consistent protection, your continual presence.

To you belongs glory, honor, praise and obedience for you are perfect in personality, complete in character, marvelous in ministry, powerful in performance and illogical in love, giving us the opposite of what we deserve.

I praise you, bask in your love, revel in your goodness, rejoice in your patience, celebrate your acceptance and rest in your forgiveness. Today I bow before you in awe, surrendering whole-heartedly, to rise up in obedience and go forth in joy, all because of your infinite greatness. To you be glory today in all I do and say, think and feel, desire and do. Amen.

Appendix C Praying On the Armor of Ephesians 6:10-18[22]

In obedience to your Word, Lord Jesus, I want *to be strong in you and the power of your might* today. I surrender afresh to you, confessing the depravity of my flesh (old nature): my tendency to rebellion and unbelief and all that flows from them, such as selfishness, pride, complaining, impatience, laziness, lust and greed, to name a few. I ask your forgiveness for these and receive it with joy.

I then ask for *the filling of your Spirit* for today: fill me to overflowing so that those who meet me will meet you, too, and know that it is you. I make you my Captain and Navigator, agreeing to obey as you lead. May I be strong in your power; may I be useful, glorifying you and bringing you pleasure. I praise you now for what you will do.

Guide me now in *praying through my day*. Go before me, empower and guide me in the things that will come, like this quiet time, and in the activities of today…[pray about the events you know will come]."

Help me to *put on and keep on the whole armor of God*, recognizing the wiles of the Devil (my weaknesses) and standing against them in your power and protection. Help me to see them before I fall into them; and if I do stumble into one, to immediately get out.

Help me to *remember that I fight not against people*, but against spiritual forces in heavenly places. Help me to fight the right enemy with the right weapons: praise, prayer and persistence in obedience, doing what I know to be right.

Help me to *put on the whole armor of God every day* so that I might be able to stand in the evil day and having done your all, to stand.

Help me to stand therefore having on **the belt of truth**, remembering that what I actually deserve is suffering, pain, death, failure and hell, exclusion from all that is good.

In contrast, you have called me to yourself, cleansed and transformed me, claimed me as your child, commissioned me to special service. You cherish me richly, deeply, wholeheartedly and consistently. In you I am dearly loved, deeply cared for, doted on and delighted in. Praise you that you have given me the exact opposite of what I deserve: making me your child, giving me an intimate relationship with you which is full of

---

[22] Taken from my book, *Equipped: Ready for Every Day Spiritual Warfare*

love, joy, peace, patience, hope, meaning, a future and protection. What joy, what grace, what a privilege, what a pleasure it is to be your child. Help me to ever stand in awe of your grace as you continually give me the exact opposite of what I deserve.

Help me to put on **the breastplate of righteousness** today: forgiving, accepting and loving myself as you do me. There is a constant level of disapproval, disappointment and disagreement within me about myself, along with the disapproval of me by others. But in you I can reject that which is based on my perfectionistic, performance-based, critical spirit, as well as that of others; I can forgive myself and rest in who I am in you: your beloved son, forgiven, accepted, cherished and sung over with joy!

Help me to put on **the shoes of peace**, rejecting the desire for revenge and the "right" to be critical of others. Help me to forgive and accept them as you do me, desiring blessing, success and joy for them as you do for me. I think of those who oppose me, who have hurt me, unjustly accused me. I again affirm my forgiveness of them now, letting go of what bothers me and praying for their blessing, success and joy.

Help me to take up, above all these, **the shield of faith** by praising you in and for all things, thereby quenching the fiery darts of the wicked one—including those negative thoughts and feelings he loves to use against me. Help me to offer the sacrifice of thanksgiving, to praise consistently and immediately, rather than first indulging in a little anger, self-pity or destructive self-centered thinking.

Help me to put on **the helmet of salvation**, remembering that in the salvation you have given me, you have included all the security and significance I will ever need. These all flow from your character and your provision, not my performance. "My salvation and my honor depend on God; he is my mighty rock, my refuge." (Ps. 62:7) I can rest in who you are and what you declare, in spite of what I--or others--may think or feel about me.

Help me to take up **the sword of the Spirit**, your Word, valuing it by reading, memorizing and meditating on it; then submitting to it, thinking it, living in it, obeying it, sharing it. I agree with you that it is sufficient for guidance, direction, protection and light. I praise you for how you help, strengthen and guide me through it.

Having on the armor, help me to then *be a person of prayer,* standing in the gap, joining you in what you are doing. I praise you, Lord, for all that you are and what you are doing in the world today. Give me discernment to see the part you have for me, primarily through prayer, and to eagerly and joyfully fulfill it.

Praise be to you for how you are going to answer this prayer, as prayer is the act of joining you in what you are doing in and through my life today. Amen.